100 MOST IMPORTANT BIBLE VERSES FOR DEALING WITH DIFFICULT PEOPLE

SMITH FREEMAN Publishing

Table of Contents by Topic

A Message to Readers

God has given us a book of promises that can guide us across the mountaintops and through the valleys of life. The Bible is a priceless gift, an infallible tool that the Lord intends for us to use every day of our lives, in good times *and* in tough times.

This book contains one hundred essential Bible verses that will help readers deal with difficult people while staying faithful to the teachings contained in God's holy Word. If you're dealing with someone who possesses an unfortunate personality—someone who makes you anxious, uncomfortable, angry, or worse—the ideas on these pages will provide wisdom, courage, and practical advice for managing that relationship. Whether you're at work, at home, or anyplace in between, the lessons in this text will give you direction and hope. When you weave God's message into the fabric of your day—and into the realities of your everyday relationships—you'll quickly discover that God's Word has the power to change everything, including your outlook and your responses.

If you're searching for better ways to deal with the difficult people in your life, the Bible verses in this text are essential. So don't give up and don't give in. Instead, keep searching for direction—God's direction. And while you're at it, keep searching for perspective and wisdom, starting with God's wisdom. When you do, you'll discover the comfort, the power, the wisdom, and the peace that only He can give.

SEVEN HELPFUL STRATEGIES FOR DEALING WITH DIFFICULT PEOPLE

All of us can be difficult to deal with at times. And all of us, from time to time, encounter folks who behave in the same way, or worse. If you have occasion to deal with difficult people (and you will), the following tips should help:

1. Understand the Personality Style of the Person You're Dealing With. When it comes to the delicate art of dealing with difficult people, knowledge is power. When you gain a better understanding of the other person's behavior patterns and motivations, you'll be better prepared to offer the best possible response (Proverbs 16:16).

2. Examine Your Own Actions and Be Certain That You're Not the One Who's Being Difficult. Take a moment to reflect on your own behavior. Perhaps the problems that concern you have their origin, at least partially, within your own heart. If so, fix yourself first (Philippians 2:3).

3. Don't Become Caught Up in the Other Person's Emotional Outbursts. If someone is ranting, raving, or worse, you have the absolute right to get up and leave. Remember: emotions are highly contagious, so if the other person is angry, you will soon become angry too. Instead of adding your own emotional energy to the outburst, you should make the conscious effort to remain calm—and part of remaining calm may be leaving the scene of the argument (Proverbs 22:24–25).

4. Don't Lecture. Lectures inevitably devolve into nagging; nagging creates animosity; animosity breeds conflict, not lasting change. Since longwinded lectures usually create more problems than they solve, save your breath (Proverbs 15:1).

5. Insist on Logical Consequences to Irresponsible Behavior. When you protect other people from the consequences of their misbehavior, you're doing those folks a profound disservice. Most people don't learn new behaviors until the old behaviors stop working, so don't be an enabler (Hebrews 12:5–6).

6. Stand Up for Yourself. If you're being mistreated, either physically, emotionally, or professionally, it's time to start taking better care of yourself. But remember that standing up for yourself doesn't require an angry outburst on your part. It's better to stand up for yourself in a calm, mature, resolute manner. And you should do so sooner rather than later (Psalm 27:1).

7: Be Quick to Forgive. If you can't find it in your heart to forgive those who have hurt you, you're hurting yourself more than you're hurting them. But remember: forgiveness should not be confused with enabling. Even after you've forgiven the difficult person in your life, you are not compelled to accept continued mistreatment from him or her (Matthew 6:14–15).

1

ACCEPTING ADVICE

BE OPEN TO ADVICE

Get all the advice and instruction you can,
so you will be wise the rest of your life.
PROVERBS 19:20 NLT

If you're dealing with a difficult person—or if you find yourself caught up in an unhealthy relationship—it's time to start searching for knowledgeable friends and mentors who can give you solid advice. Why do you need help evaluating your own situation? Because you're probably too close to the situation and to the person you see in the mirror, that's why. Sometimes you'll be tempted to give yourself straight *A*'s when you deserve considerably lower grades. On other occasions, you may become your own worst critic, giving yourself a string of failing marks when you deserve better. The truth, of course, is usually somewhere in between.

Finding a wise mentor is only half the battle. It takes just as much wisdom—and sometimes more—to act upon good advice as it does to give it. So find people you can trust, listen to them carefully, and act accordingly. When you do, you'll quickly discover that your mentors have dealt with difficult people and learned lessons that can help you survive and thrive.

More Thoughts about Advice: Giving It and Accepting It

God guides through the counsel of good people.
E. Stanley Jones

It takes a wise person to give good advice,
but an even wiser person to take it.
Marie T. Freeman

A single word, if spoken
in a friendly spirit, may be sufficient
to turn one from dangerous error.
Fanny Crosby

The next best thing to being wise oneself
is to live in a circle of those who are.
C. S. Lewis

The effective mentor strives to help
a man or woman discover
what they can be in Christ
and then holds them accountable
to become that person.
Howard Hendricks

More from God's Word

The wise are glad to be instructed.
PROVERBS 10:8 NLT

*He whose ear listens to the life-giving
reproof will dwell among the wise.*
PROVERBS 15:31 NASB

*How much better is it to
get wisdom than gold!
and to get understanding
rather to be chosen than silver!*
PROVERBS 16:16 KJV

*Plans fail when there is no counsel,
but with many advisers they succeed.*
PROVERBS 15:22 HCSB

*Spend time with the wise
and you will become wise,
but the friends of fools will suffer.*
PROVERBS 13:20 NCV

A Timely Tip

If you're experiencing tough times, don't keep everything bottled up inside. Find a person you can really trust, and talk things over. A second opinion (or, for that matter, a third, fourth, or fifth opinion) is usually helpful.

2

ACCEPTING THE SITUATION

YES, YOU'RE GOING TO ENCOUNTER DIFFICULT PEOPLE, AND THAT'S OKAY

*Should we accept only good things from
the hand of God and never anything bad?*

JOB 2:10 NLT

Unless you're living like a modern-day hermit, you're going to encounter difficult people. Lots of them. Why? Because people with difficult personalities are everywhere. They're in all walks of life, in all economic strata, in every profession, and in every large institution. Typically, you don't invite these individuals to hijack your day or your life. They simply show up, sometimes out of nowhere, making you and everybody around you feel slightly uncomfortable, or worse. Sometimes difficult people arrive in a hurry and leave just as quickly. When they do, you breathe a sigh of relief. But sometimes these folks are permanent members of your friend group or family. You can avoid them, but you can't escape them.

The ideas in this book are intended to help you navigate difficult personal relationships without compromising your ethics, losing your sanity, or neglecting your faith. So instead of fretting about the prickly personalities who inhabit your life, open your heart to

God's guidance and His love.

If you're encountering unfortunate circumstances that are beyond your control right now, accept those circumstances. And trust God. When you do, you can be comforted in the knowledge that your Creator is good, that His love endures forever, and that He understands His plans perfectly, even when you do not.

More Thoughts about Acceptance

Acceptance says, "True, this is my situation at the moment. I'll look unblinkingly at the reality of it. But, I'll also open my hands to accept willingly whatever a loving Father sends."
Catherine Marshall

One of the marks of spiritual maturity is the quiet confidence that God is in control, without the need to understand why He does what He does.
Charles Swindoll

Christians who are strong in the faith grow as they accept whatever God allows to enter their lives.
Billy Graham

Loving Him means the thankful acceptance of all things that His love has appointed.
Elisabeth Elliot

Accept each day as it comes to you. Do not waste your time and energy wishing for a different set of circumstances.
Sarah Young

More from God's Word

*Trust in the LORD with all your heart
and lean not on your own understanding.*
PROVERBS 3:5 NIV

*Everything God made is good, and nothing
should be refused if it is accepted with thanks.*
1 TIMOTHY 4:4 NCV

He is the LORD. He will do what He thinks is good.
1 SAMUEL 3:18 HCSB

*Now everything is from God, who reconciled
us to Himself through Christ
and gave us the ministry of reconciliation.*
2 CORINTHIANS 5:18 HCSB

*For the Yahweh is good, and His love is eternal;
His faithfulness endures through all generations.*
PSALM 100:5 HCSB

A Timely Tip

Try though you might, you simply cannot change another person's personality. So whenever you encounter people or situations that you cannot change, you must learn the wisdom of acceptance. Learn to trust God in every circumstance, especially the difficult circumstances—and the difficult people—you cannot change.

3

ACTION:
DON'T PROCRASTINATE

YOU'RE NOT STUCK

Therefore, with your minds ready for action,
be serious and set your hope completely on the grace
to be brought to you at the revelation of Jesus Christ.
1 PETER 1:13 HCSB

If you're trying to deal with a difficult person—or if you're trying to navigate a challenging relationship—you may, at times, become discouraged or angry or both. If so, you are not alone. Dealing with other people is a universal problem that we all face from time to time. And because it's a difficult problem to solve, we're tempted to postpone action or to simply ignore the pain as best we can, hoping that things will improve on their own. But procrastination is seldom the best solution, and neither is denial. A far better solution, of course, is to learn better ways to respond to the difficult person, and then to ask God for the strength to respond wisely and courageously.

The ideas in this text will be useful to you *if* you employ them. So if you'd like to deal more effectively with difficult people, keep reading and ask God to give you the courage to do the right thing, even when it's hard. And while you're at it, remember that you're not stuck *unless* you allow yourself to be stuck.

MORE THOUGHTS ABOUT DOING IT NOW

Pray as though everything depended on God.
Work as though everything depended on you.
ST. AUGUSTINE

Action springs not from thought,
but from a readiness for responsibility.
DIETRICH BONHOEFFER

The one word in the spiritual vocabulary is now.
OSWALD CHAMBERS

There's some task which the God of all the universe,
the great Creator, has for you to do,
and which will remain undone and incomplete,
until by faith and obedience,
you step into the will of God.
ALAN REDPATH

Authentic faith cannot help but act.
BETH MOORE

More from God's Word

But prove yourselves doers of the word,
and not merely hearers who delude themselves.
James 1:22 NASB

When you make a vow to God,
do not delay in fulfilling it.
He has no pleasure in fools; fulfill your vow.
Ecclesiastes 5:4 NIV

For the kingdom of God is not a matter of talk but of power.
1 Corinthians 4:20 HCSB

Whenever we have the opportunity, we should do good
to everyone—especially to those in the family of faith.
Galatians 6:10 NLT

Well done, good and faithful servant;
you were faithful over a few things,
I will make you ruler over many things.
Enter into the joy of your lord.
Matthew 25:21 NKJV

A Timely Tip

If you've been putting off dealing with a difficult person or an uncomfortable situation, pray for God's wisdom and His strength. Ask Him to help you deal with the situation in the best way possible, which usually means responding sooner rather than later.

4

ADVERSITY

TOUGH TIMES NEVER LAST, TOUGH PEOPLE DO

God blesses the people who patiently endure testing and temptation.
Afterward they will receive the crown of life
that God has promised to those who love him.
JAMES 1:12 NLT

The times that try men and women's souls are also the times when character is forged on the anvil of adversity. But the character building is never easy. Surviving a difficult relationship requires courage, strength, prayer, and insight.

During difficult times, we are tempted to complain, to worry, to blame other people, and to do little else. Usually complaints and worries change nothing; intelligent action, on the other hand, can change everything.

If you find yourself enduring difficult circumstances—or if you're confounded by someone with a problematic personality—remember that God remains in His heaven. If you become discouraged with the direction of your day or your life, turn your thoughts and prayers to Him. He is a God of possibility, not negativity. He will guide you through your difficulties and beyond them. And then, with a renewed spirit of optimism and hope, you can thank the Giver of all things good for gifts that are simply too profound to fully understand and for treasures that are too numerous to count.

MORE THOUGHTS ABOUT ADVERSITY

God alone can give us songs in the night.
C. H. SPURGEON

*God is in control. He may not
take away trials or make detours for us,
but He strengthens us through them.*
BILLY GRAHAM

*Often God has to shut a door
in our face so that He can subsequently
open the door through which He wants us to go.*
CATHERINE MARSHALL

*Human problems are
never greater than divine solutions.*
ERWIN LUTZER

*Life is literally filled with
God-appointed storms.
These squalls surge across everyone's horizon.
We all need them.*
CHARLES SWINDOLL

More from God's Word

We are hard-pressed on every side,
yet not crushed; we are perplexed,
but not in despair.
2 Corinthians 4:8 NKJV

He heals the brokenhearted and binds up their wounds.
Psalm 147:3 HCSB

I called to the Lord in my distress;
I called to my God. From His temple He heard my voice.
2 Samuel 22:7 HCSB

The Lord is my rock, my fortress,
and my deliverer, my God,
my mountain where I seek refuge.
My shield, the horn of my salvation,
my stronghold, my refuge, and my Savior.
2 Samuel 22:2–3 HCSB

The Lord is my shepherd; I shall not want.
Psalm 23:1 KJV

A Timely Tip

Perhaps because of a relationship with a difficult person, you're being forced to step outside your comfort zone. If so, consider it an opportunity to grow spiritually and emotionally. Your challenge is to trust yourself, to trust God, and to follow His lead.

5

ANGER

DON'T LET ANGER
DOMINATE YOUR THOUGHTS

Everyone must be quick to hear, slow to speak, and slow to anger, for man's anger does not accomplish God's righteousness.
JAMES 1:19–20 HCSB

If you're engaged in an ongoing relationship with a difficult person, you probably know a thing or two (or three) about anger. After all, everybody gets mad occasionally, and you're probably no exception.

Anger is a natural human emotion that is sometimes necessary and appropriate. Even Jesus became angry when confronted with the moneychangers in the temple (Matthew 21). Righteous indignation is an appropriate response to evil, but God does not intend that anger should rule our lives. Far from it. That's why Proverbs 16:32 states, "Controlling your temper is better than capturing a city" (NCV).

If you've allowed anger to become a regular visitor at your house, you should pray for wisdom, for patience, and for a heart that is so filled with forgiveness that it contains no room for bitterness. God will help you control your temper if you ask Him— and that's a good thing because anger and peace cannot coexist in the same mind. So obey God's Word by turning away from anger today and every day. You'll be glad you did, and so will your family and friends.

More Thoughts about Anger

Life is too short to spend it being angry, bored, or dull.
BARBARA JOHNSON

Frustration is not the will of God.
There is time to do anything and everything
that God wants us to do.
ELISABETH ELLIOT

Hot heads and cold hearts never solved anything.
BILLY GRAHAM

Anger and bitterness—
whatever the cause—
only end up hurting us.
Turn that anger over to Christ.
BILLY GRAHAM

Hence it is not enough to deal with the temper.
We must go to the source,
and change the inmost nature,
and the angry humors will die away of themselves.
HENRY DRUMMOND

More from God's Word

But I tell you that anyone who is angry
with a brother or sister will be subject to judgment.
MATTHEW 5:22 NIV

But now you must also put away
all the following: anger, wrath, malice, slander,
and filthy language from your mouth.
COLOSSIANS 3:8 HCSB

He who is slow to wrath has great understanding,
but he who is impulsive exalts folly.
PROVERBS 14:29 NKJV

A hot-tempered man stirs up conflict,
but a man slow to anger calms strife.
PROVERBS 15:18 HCSB

Do not let the sun go down on your anger,
and do not give the devil an opportunity.
EPHESIANS 4:26–27 NASB

A Timely Tip

Don't be caught up in another person's emotional outbursts. Emotions are highly contagious and angry encounters seldom have happy endings. So if someone is ranting, raving, or worse, you have the right to leave the scene of the argument.

6

ARGUMENTS

ARGUMENTS:
DON'T WASTE YOUR BREATH

Avoiding a fight is a mark of honor;
only fools insist on quarreling.
PROVERBS 20:3 NLT

Time and again, God's Word warns us against angry outbursts and needless arguments. Arguments are seldom won but often lost, so when we acquire the unfortunate habit of habitual bickering, we do harm to our friends, to our families, to our coworkers, and to ourselves. And when we engage in petty squabbles, our losses usually outpace our gains.

If you're dealing with a difficult person, you may be tempted to "take the bait" and argue about matters great and small. If you find yourself in this predicament, take a deep breath, say a silent prayer, and calm yourself down. In dealing with difficult people, arguments are a monumental waste of time and energy. Since you'll never win the argument anyway, there's no rational reason to participate.

More Thoughts about Arguments

*An argument seldom convinces anyone
contrary to his inclinations.*
Thomas Fuller

Never persist in trying to set people right.
Hannah Whitall Smith

*Most serious conflicts evolve from
our attempts to control others
who will not accept our control.*
William Glasser

Argument is the worst sort of conversation.
Jonathan Swift

*Whatever you do when conflicts arise,
be wise. Fight against jumping
to quick conclusions and seeing
only your side. There are always two sides
on the streets of conflict. Look both ways.*
Charles Swindoll

More from God's Word

Do everything without grumbling and arguing,
so that you may be blameless and pure.
PHILIPPIANS 2:14-15 HCSB

A soft answer turneth away wrath:
but grievous words stir up anger.
PROVERBS 15:1 KJV

If any man among you seem to be religious,
and bridleth not his tongue, but deceiveth his own heart,
this man's religion is vain.
JAMES 1:26 KJV

I tell you that on the day of judgment
people will have to account for every careless word
they speak. For by your words you will be acquitted,
and by your words you will be condemned.
MATTHEW 12:36–37 HCSB

People with quick tempers cause trouble,
but those who control their tempers stop a quarrel.
PROVERBS 15:18 NCV

A Timely Tip

Arguments usually cause many more problems than they solve. And if you're dealing with a difficult person, you probably won't win the argument anyway. So don't be afraid to leave the scene of an argument rather than engage in a debate that cannot be won.

7

Asking God for Help

Ask God for the Help You Need to Deal with Difficult People

Ask, and it will be given to you; seek, and you will find;
knock, and it will be opened to you.
For everyone who asks receives, and he who seeks finds,
and to him who knocks it will be opened.

MATTHEW 7:7–8 NASB

If you're dealing with a difficult person, you need God's help. And if you ask Him, He will most certainly provide the help you need. But don't expect Him to do all the work. When you do your part, He will do His part—and when He does, you can expect good things to happen.

The Bible promises that God will guide you if you let Him. Your job is to let Him. But sometimes you will be tempted to do otherwise. Sometimes you'll be tempted to respond impulsively to another person's bad behavior. But if you impulsively strike back, you'll probably strike out. A far better strategy, of course, is to pray for God's wisdom and His peace.

The Lord has promised that when you ask for His help, He will not withhold it. So ask. Ask Him to lead you, to protect you, and to correct you. Ask for His guidance in difficult situations. Then trust the answers He gives.

God stands at the door and waits. When you knock, He opens. When you ask, He answers. Your task, of course, to make God a full partner in every aspect of your life—and to seek His guidance prayerfully, confidently, and often.

MORE THOUGHTS ABOUT ASKING GOD FOR HELP

God will help us become the people we are meant to be, if only we will ask Him.
HANNAH WHITALL SMITH

God insists that we ask, not because He needs to know our situation, but because we need the spiritual discipline of asking.
CATHERINE MARSHALL

It's important that you keep asking God to show you what He wants you to do. If you don't ask, you won't know.
STORMIE OMARTIAN

Are you serious about wanting God's guidance to become a personal reality in your life? The first step is to tell God that you know you can't manage your own life; that you need His help.
CATHERINE MARSHALL

More from God's Word

Until now you have asked for nothing
in My name. Ask and you will receive,
so that your joy may be complete.
JOHN 16:24 HCSB

Your Father knows the things
you have need of before you ask Him.
MATTHEW 6:8 NKJV

Do not be anxious about anything,
but in everything, by prayer and petition,
with thanksgiving, present your requests to God.
PHILIPPIANS 4:6 NIV

The effective prayer of a righteous man can accomplish much.
JAMES 5:16 NASB

You did not choose me, but I chose you
and appointed you so that you might go and bear fruit—
fruit that will last—and so that whatever
you ask in my name the Father will give you.
JOHN 15:16 NIV

A Timely Tip

If you're dealing with a difficult person, it's always the right time to ask for God's help. If you have questions, He has answers. So when in doubt, pray. And keep praying until the answer arrives.

8

ASSURANCE

DRAW QUIET CONFIDENCE FROM GOD

*Let us hold tightly without wavering to the hope we affirm,
for God can be trusted to keep his promise.*

HEBREWS 10:23 NLT

If you've been emotionally battered by a person with a difficult personality, your confidence may have been shaken. If so, God wants you to reclaim the confidence and assurance that can—and should—be yours. As a Christian, you have many reasons to be confident. After all, God is in His heaven; Christ has risen; and you are the recipient of God's grace. Despite these blessings, you may, from time to time, find yourself being tormented by negative emotions—and you are certainly not alone.

Even the most faithful Christians are overcome by occasional bouts of fear and discouragement. You are no different. Every life— including yours—is a series of successes and failures, celebrations and disappointments, joys and sorrows, hopes and doubts.

But even when you feel very distant from God, remember that God is never distant from you. When you sincerely seek His presence, He will touch your heart, calm your fears, and restore your confidence. He can help you deal with a difficult person, or help you do anything else for that matter. No challenge is too big for Him.

More Thoughts about Assurance

Never yield to gloomy anticipation.
Place your hope and confidence in God.
He has no record of failure.
Lettie Cowman

Faith and obedience are bound up
in the same bundle. He that obeys God,
trusts God; and he that trusts God, obeys God.
C. H. Spurgeon

One of the marks of spiritual maturity
is the quiet confidence that God is in control,
without the need to understand why He does what He does.
Charles Swindoll

When a train goes through a tunnel
and it gets dark, you don't throw away your ticket
and jump off. You sit still and trust the engineer.
Corrie ten Boom

Never be afraid to trust an unknown future to a known God.
Corrie ten Boom

More from God's Word

For this is the secret: Christ lives in you.
This gives you assurance of sharing his glory.
Colossians 1:27 NLT

In quietness and in confidence shall be your strength.
Isaiah 30:15 KJV

Let us draw near with a true heart in full assurance
of faith, our hearts sprinkled clean from an
evil conscience and our bodies washed in pure water.
Hebrews 10:22 HCSB

As for God, his way is perfect: the word of the Lord is tried:
he is a buckler to all those that trust in him.
Psalm 18:30 KJV

For our gospel came not unto you in word only, but also
in power, and in the Holy Ghost, and in much assurance.
1 Thessalonians 1:5 KJV

A Timely Tip

If a person with a difficult personality has caused you to doubt your abilities or to place unreasonable limits on your opportunities, it's time for a complete mental makeover. God created you for a purpose, and He has important work specifically designed for you. So don't let anyone steal your joy, your self-confidence, or your faith in God.

9

ATTITUDE

MAINTAIN THE
RIGHT KIND OF ATTITUDE

You must have the same attitude
that Christ Jesus had.
PHILIPPIANS 2:5 NLT

Attitudes are the mental filters through which we view and interpret the world around us. People with positive attitudes look for the best and usually find it. People burdened by chronically negative attitudes are not so fortunate.

If you're dealing with a difficult person, your attitude will be affected. Your job, simply put, is to minimize the damage to your psyche. Your attitude will inevitably determine the quality and direction of your day and your life. That's why it's so important to stay positive.

The Christian life can, and should, be cause for celebration. After all, every new day is a gift, every new circumstance an opportunity to praise and to serve. So how will you direct your thoughts today? Will you focus on God's love? Will you hold fast to His promises and trust His plan for your life? Or will you allow your thoughts to be hijacked by negativity and doubt? If you're a thoughtful believer, you'll think optimistically about yourself and your future.

And while you're at it, you'll give thanks to the Creator for more blessings than you can possibly count.

More Thoughts about Attitude

*When we get rid of inner conflicts
and wrong attitudes toward life,
we will almost automatically burst into joy.*
E. Stanley Jones

*The things we think are the things that feed our souls.
If we think on pure and lovely things, we shall grow pure
and lovely like them; and the converse is equally true.*
Hannah Whitall Smith

*Developing a positive attitude means
working continually to find
what is uplifting and encouraging.*
Barbara Johnson

*We choose what attitudes we have right now.
And it's a continuing choice.*
John Maxwell

*The longer I live the more convinced
I become that life is 10 percent what happens
to us and 90 percent how we respond to it.*
Charles Swindoll

More from God's Word

Finally, brothers, rejoice. Become mature,
be encouraged, be of the same mind,
be at peace, and the God of love
and peace will be with you.
2 Corinthians 13:11 HCSB

Rejoice always; pray without ceasing.
1 Thessalonians 5:16–17 NASB

A merry heart makes a cheerful countenance.
Proverbs 15:13 NKJV

Be glad and rejoice,
because your reward is great in heaven.
Matthew 5:12 HCSB

This is the day the Lord has made;
let us rejoice and be glad in it.
Psalm 118:24 HCSB

A Timely Tip

Difficult people have a way of hijacking your thoughts and derailing your emotions. When an encounter with a difficult person threatens to disrupt your day—or your life—step back from the situation, take a deep breath, say a short prayer, and remind yourself that this, too, will pass. Then ask God to help you do whatever is required to regain your sense of optimism and hope.

10

BIBLE STUDY

DIG DEEP INTO GOD'S WORD

All scripture is given by inspiration of God,
and is profitable for doctrine, for reproof,
for correction, for instruction in righteousness.
2 TIMOTHY 3:16 KJV

If you're dealing with a difficult person or an unhealthy relationship, there's a book for that. It's called the Holy Bible. God's Word is unlike any other book. The words of Matthew 4:4 remind us, "Man shall not live by bread alone, but by every word that proceedeth out of the mouth of God" (KJV).

As believers, we are instructed to study the Bible and meditate upon its meaning for our lives, yet far too many Bibles are laid aside by well-intentioned believers who would like to study the Bible if they could "just find the time."

Warren Wiersbe observed, "When the child of God looks into the Word of God, he sees the Son of God. And, he is transformed by the Spirit of God to share in the glory of God." God's holy Word is, indeed, a transforming, life-changing, one-of-a-kind treasure. And it's up to you—and only you—to use it that way.

More Thoughts about Bible Study

Do you want your faith to grow? Then let the Bible
begin to saturate your mind and soul.
BILLY GRAHAM

Gather the riches of God's promises.
Nobody can take away from you those texts from
the Bible which you have learned by heart.
CORRIE TEN BOOM

Reading the Bible has a purifying effect upon your life.
Let nothing take the place of this daily exercise.
BILLY GRAHAM

Read the scripture, not only as history,
but as a love letter sent to you from God.
THOMAS WATSON

I believe the reason so many are failing today is that they have
not disciplined themselves to read God's Word consistently, day
in and day out, and to apply it to every situation in life.
KAY ARTHUR

More from God's Word

The counsel of the LORD stands forever,
the plans of His heart from generation to generation.
PSALM 33:11 NASB

But grow in the grace and knowledge
of our Lord and Savior Jesus Christ.
To Him be the glory both now and to the day of eternity.
2 PETER 3:18 HCSB

But the word of the Lord endures forever.
And this is the word that was preached as the gospel to you.
1 PETER 1:25 HCSB

But whoever looks intently into
the perfect law that gives freedom,
and continues in it—not forgetting
what they have heard, but doing it—
they will be blessed in what they do.
JAMES 1:25 NIV

You will be a good servant of Christ Jesus,
nourished by the words of the faith
and of the good teaching that you have followed.
1 TIMOTHY 4:6 HCSB

A TIMELY TIP

The Bible is God's guidebook for every situation you'll ever face. And even if you've studied the Bible for many years, you've still got lots to learn. Bible study should be a lifelong endeavor. Make it *your* lifelong endeavor.

11

BITTERNESS

DON'T GIVE IN TO BITTERNESS

*Let all bitterness, wrath, anger, clamor,
and evil speaking be put away from you, with all malice.
And be kind to one another, tenderhearted,
forgiving one another, even as God in Christ forgave you.*
EPHESIANS 4:31–32 NKJV

If you've been dealing with a difficult person for an extended period of time, you may have become bitter. If so, be forewarned: bitterness is a spiritual sickness. It will consume your soul; it is dangerous to your emotional health; it can destroy you if you let it. So don't let it!

The world holds few if any rewards for those who remain angrily focused upon the shortcomings of others. Still, the act of forgiveness is difficult for all but the most saintly men and women. Being frail, fallible, imperfect human beings, most of us are quick to anger, quick to blame, slow to forgive, and even slower to forget. Yet we know that it's best to forgive others, just as we, too, have been forgiven.

If there exists even one person—including yourself—against whom you still harbor bitter feelings, it's time to forgive and move on. Bitterness and regret are not part of God's plan for you, but God won't force you to forgive others. It's a job that only you can do, and the sooner you do it, the better.

If you are caught up in intense feelings of anger or resentment, you know all too well the destructive power of these emotions. How can you rid yourself of these feelings? First, you must prayerfully ask God to cleanse your heart. Then, you must learn to catch yourself whenever thoughts of bitterness or hatred begin to attack you. Your challenge is this: you must learn to resist negative thoughts before they hijack your emotions. When you learn to direct your thoughts toward more positive topics, you'll be protected from the spiritual and emotional consequences of bitterness. And you'll be wiser, healthier, and happier too.

MORE THOUGHTS ABOUT THE DANGERS OF BITTERNESS

Bitterness sentences you to relive the hurt over and over.
LEE STROBEL

Bitterness is anger gone sour, an attitude of deep discontent that poisons our souls and destroys our peace.
BILLY GRAHAM

Bitterness is a spiritual cancer, a rapidly growing malignancy that can consume your life. Bitterness cannot be ignored but must be healed at the very core, and only Christ can heal bitterness.
BETH MOORE

More from God's Word

Do all things without complaining and disputing,
that you may become blameless and harmless,
children of God without fault in the midst
of a crooked and perverse generation,
among whom you shine as lights in the world.
PHILIPPIANS 2:14–15 NKJV

The heart knows its own bitterness,
and a stranger does not share its joy.
PROVERBS 14:10 NKJV

But when you are praying,
first forgive anyone you are holding
a grudge against, so that your Father in heaven
will forgive your sins, too.
MARK 11:25 NLT

Do not judge, and you will not be judged.
Do not condemn, and you will not be condemned.
Forgive, and you will be forgiven.
LUKE 6:37 HCSB

A Timely Tip

The Bible warns that bitterness is both dangerous and self-destructive. So today, make a list of the people you need to forgive and the things you need to forget. Then ask God to give you the strength to forgive, to forget, and to move on.

12

BLAME

DON'T PLAY THE BLAME GAME

The heart knows its own bitterness,
and a stranger does not share its joy.
PROVERBS 14:10 NKJV

When you're dealing with a person who possesses a difficult personality, it's easy to become angry; it's easy to be hurt; and it's easy to cast blame. Why? Because blaming is much easier than fixing, and criticizing others is so much easier than dealing forthrightly with the issues at hand. So instead of attempting to resolve the problematic relationship legitimately by confronting the issues head-on, we are inclined to fret, to blame, and to criticize, while doing precious little else. When we do, the problematic relationship, quite predictably, remains troubled.

Some relationships are so destructive that they need to be ended permanently. But other relationships can be repaired. However, casting blame doesn't usually do much to repair broken relationships. So as you consider your relationships with the difficult people who populate your life, remember that the blame game is a game that nobody wins.

More Thoughts about Blaming Others

You'll never win the blame game, so why even bother to play?
MARIE T. FREEMAN

*Man must cease attributing his problems
to his environment, and learn again
to exercise his will—his personal responsibility
in the realm of faith and morals.*
ALBERT SCHWEITZER

*Make no excuses. Rationalize nothing.
Blame no one. Humble yourself.*
BETH MOORE

*Do not think of the faults of others
but what is good in them and faulty in yourself.*
ST. TERESA OF AVILA

*Bear with the faults of others as
you would have them bear with yours.*
PHILLIPS BROOKS

More from God's Word

*People's own foolishness ruins their lives,
but in their minds they blame the LORD.*
PROVERBS 19:3 NCV

Therefore, laying aside falsehood,
speak truth each one you with his neighbor,
for we are members of one another.
EPHESIANS 4:25 NASB

All bitterness, anger and wrath,
shouting and slander must be removed from you,
along with all malice. And be kind
and compassionate to one another,
forgiving one another,
just as God also forgave you in Christ.
EPHESIANS 4:31–32 HCSB

But each person should examine his own work,
and then he will have a reason for boasting
in himself alone, and not in respect to someone else.
For each person will have to carry his own load.
GALATIANS 6:4–5 HCSB

Don't let your spirit rush to be angry,
for anger abides in the heart of fools.
ECCLESIASTES 7:9 HCSB

A TIMELY TIP

Blame focuses your mind on the negative aspects of your life. So learn to count your blessings, not your misfortunes. And while you're at it, remember that you can't ever win the blame game, so don't play.

13

BLESSINGS

FOCUS ON BLESSINGS, NOT BURDENS

Blessings crown the head of the righteous.
PROVERBS 10:6 NIV

When you're dealing with a difficult person, it's easy to focus on your problems, not your blessings. A far better strategy, of course, is to focus on your blessings, not your burdens.

If you tried to count all your blessings, how long would it take? A very, very long time. After all, you've been given the priceless gift of life here on earth and the promise of life eternal in heaven. And you've been given so much more.

Billy Graham noted: "We should think of the blessings we so easily take for granted: life itself; preservation from danger; every bit of health we enjoy; every hour of liberty; the ability to see, to hear, to speak, to think, and to imagine, all this comes from the hand of God." That's sound advice for believers—followers of the One from Galilee—who have so much to be thankful for.

Your blessings, all of which are gifts from above, are indeed too numerous to count, but it never hurts to begin counting them anyway. Even when times are tough, it's always the right time to say thanks to the Giver for the gifts you can count, and all the other ones too.

More Thoughts about God's Blessings

We do not need to beg Him to bless us;
He simply cannot help it.
HANNAH WHITALL SMITH

God's gifts put men's best dreams to shame.
ELIZABETH BARRETT BROWNING

God is the giver, and we are the receivers.
And His richest gifts are bestowed
not upon those who do the greatest things,
but upon those who accept
His abundance and His grace.
HANNAH WHITALL SMITH

God is always trying to give good things to us,
but our hands are too full to receive them.
ST. AUGUSTINE

God has promised us abundance,
peace, and eternal life.
These treasures are ours for the asking.
One of the great mysteries of life
is why so many of us wait so long
to lay claim to God's gifts.
MARIE T. FREEMAN

More from God's Word

May Yahweh bless you and protect you; may Yahweh make His face shine on you and be gracious to you.
NUMBERS 6:24–25 HCSB

The LORD is my rock, my fortress, and my deliverer, my God, my mountain where I seek refuge. My shield, the horn of my salvation, my stronghold, my refuge, and my Savior.
2 SAMUEL 22:2–3 HCSB

*You will show me the path of life;
in Your presence is fullness of joy;
at Your right hand are pleasures forevermore.*
PSALM 16:11 NKJV

*The LORD is good to all,
and his tender mercies are over all his works.*
PSALM 145:9 KJV

The LORD is my shepherd; I shall not want.
PSALM 23:1 KJV

A Timely Tip

Even if you're grappling with a difficult person or an uncomfortable situation, you are still richly blessed. In fact, God has given you more blessings than you can possibly count, but it doesn't hurt to begin counting them. And while you're at it, don't forget to praise the Giver of all those incalculable gifts.

14

BURNOUT

DON'T BURN OUT

But those who wait on the LORD shall renew their strength;
they shall mount up with wings like eagles, they shall run
and not be weary, they shall walk and not faint.
ISAIAH 40:31 NKJV

Is there a difficult person in your life who seems to be monopolizing your time? And are you having a hard time saying no to a laundry list of unreasonable requests? If so, it's time to take a long, hard look at the way you're prioritizing your days and your life.

If you don't prioritize your day, other people will. Before you know it, you'll be taking on lots of new commitments, doing many things, but doing few things well. God, on the other hand, encourages you to slow down, to quiet yourself, and to spend time with Him. And you can be sure that God's way is best.

How will you organize your life? Will you carve out quiet moments with the Creator? And while you're at it, will you focus your energies and your resources on only the most important tasks on your to-do list? Will you summon the strength to say no when it's appropriate, or will you max out your schedule, leaving much of your most important work undone?

Today, slow yourself down, commit more time to God, and spend less time on low-priority tasks. When you do, you'll be amazed at how the Father can revolutionize your life.

MORE THOUGHTS ABOUT BURNOUT

*There are many burned-out people
who think more is always better,
who deem it unspiritual to say no.*
SARAH YOUNG

*Beware of having so much to do
that you really do nothing at all
because you do not wait upon God to do it aright.*
C. H. SPURGEON

*Life is strenuous.
See that your clock does not run down.*
LETTIE COWMAN

God specializes in giving people a fresh start.
RICK WARREN

*The more comfortable we are with mystery
in our journey, the more rest
we will know along the way.*
JOHN ELDREDGE

More from God's Word

I leave you peace; my peace I give you.
I do not give it to you as the world does.
So don't let your hearts be troubled or afraid.
JOHN 14:27 NCV

But godliness with contentment is a great gain.
1 TIMOTHY 6:6 HCSB

Abundant peace belongs to those who love
Your instruction; nothing makes them stumble.
PSALM 119:165 HCSB

Don't burn out; keep yourselves fueled and aflame.
Be alert servants of the Master, cheerfully expectant.
Don't quit in hard times; pray all the harder.
ROMANS 12:11–12 MSG

Careful planning puts you ahead in the long run;
hurry and scurry puts you further behind.
PROVERBS 21:5 MSG

A Timely Tip

God can make all things new, including you. When you are exhausted from the experience of dealing with a difficult person, remember that the Lord can renew your spirit and restore your strength. Your job, of course, is to let Him.

15

CELEBRATION

CELEBRATE EVERY DAY!

Rejoice in the Lord always.
Again I will say, rejoice!
PHILIPPIANS 4:4 NKJV

Even when times are tough and the people around you are being difficult, there's still cause for celebration. Each day has its own share of burdens, but it also has its share of blessings. Our assignment, as grateful believers, is to look for the blessings and celebrate them.

Today, like every other, is a priceless gift from God. He has offered us yet another opportunity to serve Him with smiling faces and willing hands. When we do our part, He inevitably does His part, and miracles happen.

The Lord has promised to bless you and keep you, now and forever. So, don't wait for the "perfect" moment—or the sunniest day—to say thanks. Make time throughout the day to thank God for His blessings. He deserves your gratitude, and you deserve the joy of expressing it.

More Thoughts about Celebrating Life

There is not one blade of grass,
there is no color in this world
that is not intended to make us rejoice.
John Calvin

Every day we live is a priceless gift of God,
loaded with possibilities to learn something new,
to gain fresh insights.
Dale Evans Rogers

All our life is celebration to us.
We are convinced, in fact,
that God is always everywhere.
St. Clement of Alexandria

The greatest honor you can give Almighty God
is to live gladly and joyfully
because of the knowledge of His love.
Juliana of Norwich

Joy is the direct result of having God's perspective
on our daily lives and the effect of
loving our Lord enough to obey His commands
and trust His promises.
Bill Bright

More from God's Word

*Rejoice always, pray without ceasing,
in everything give thanks;
for this is the will of God in Christ Jesus for you.*
1 Thessalonians 5:16–18 NKJV

*I delight greatly in the Lord;
my soul rejoices in my God.*
Isaiah 61:10 NIV

A happy heart is like a continual feast.
Proverbs 15:15 NCV

*This is the day which the Lord has made;
let us rejoice and be glad in it.*
Psalm 118:24 NASB

*I came that they may have life,
and have it abundantly.*
John 10:10 NASB

A Timely Tip

When times are tough and people are being difficult, it's easy to become discouraged. Easy, but wrong. Even when your circumstances are difficult, you still have many reasons to celebrate. So focus on the positive aspects of life and celebrate them today and every day.

16

CHANGE

PEOPLE CHANGE WHEN THEY DECIDE TO CHANGE, NOT WHEN YOU WANT THEM TO CHANGE

*To every thing there is a season,
and a time to every purpose under the heaven.*
ECCLESIASTES 3:1 KJV

Life would be much easier if we could just snap our fingers and transform difficult people into friendly, cooperative, encouraging human beings. But it doesn't work that way. People change when they want to, not when we want them to. No matter how hard we try, we simply cannot change someone else's personality. What we can change, however, is the way we deal with the person who's being difficult.

A person with a problematic personality can ruin your day with a single sentence if you allow him (or her) to do it. Your challenge is to step back from the situation and to respond maturely, not impulsively. Of course, you may be tempted to rebuke the other person, or to try to "teach him a lesson" in hopes that he will permanently change his ways. But lectures and rebukes seldom achieve permanent results.

So, if you're really serious about reforming someone's prickly personality, don't lecture him; don't scold him; don't berate him or criticize him. Instead, pray for him. God can change any heart and transform any personality trait. You, on the other hand, cannot.

More Thoughts about
Trying to Change Other People

*Most serious conflicts evolve from
our attempts to control others
who will not accept our control.*
WILLIAM GLASSER

*When dealing with other people,
remember that you are not dealing
with creatures of logic, but with creatures of emotion.*
DALE CARNEGIE

*An argument seldom convinces anyone
contrary to his inclinations.*
THOMAS FULLER

Never persist in trying to set people right.
HANNAH WHITALL SMITH

*It's easy to manage our neighbors' business—
it's our own business that's tough.*
JOSH BILLINGS

More from God's Word

The wise see danger ahead and avoid it,
but fools keep going and get into trouble.
PROVERBS 22:3 NCV

Then He who sat on the throne said,
"Behold, I make all things new."
REVELATION 21:5 NKJV

But grow in the grace and knowledge
of our Lord and Savior Jesus Christ.
To Him be the glory both now and forever. Amen.
2 PETER 3:18 NKJV

When I was a child, I spoke like a child,
I thought like a child, I reasoned like a child.
When I became a man, I put aside childish things.
1 CORINTHIANS 13:11 HCSB

I am the LORD, and I do not change.
MALACHI 3:6 NLT

A Timely Tip

Unless the person you're trying to change is a young child, and unless you are that child's parent or guardian, don't try to change his or her personality. Why? Because people change when they want to, not when you want them to.

17

CHARACTER

DON'T COMPROMISE YOURSELF

The godly are directed by honesty.
PROVERBS 11:5 NLT

Sometimes difficult people encourage us to behave immaturely or unethically or both. On these occasions, we're tempted to focus on external forces and persuasive personalities, not on the conscience that God has placed deep within our hearts. But if we disregard that quiet inner voice, we make a profound mistake.

As believers in Christ, we must seek to live each day with discipline, honesty, and faith. When we do, at least two things happen: integrity becomes a habit, and God blesses us because of our obedience to Him.

Would you like a time-tested formula for successful living? Here is a simple formula that is proven and true: don't compromise yourself. Period.

Instead of getting lost in the crowd, seek guidance from God. Instead of giving in to the unreasonable demands of a difficult person, stand your ground. Instead of tuning out your conscience, tune in to it. Does this sound too simplistic? Perhaps it is simple, but it is also the only way to reap all the marvelous riches that God has in store for you.

MORE THOUGHTS
ABOUT CHARACTER

Let your words be the genuine picture of your heart.
JOHN WESLEY

Character is what you are in the dark.
D. L. MOODY

True greatness is not measured
by the headlines or wealth.
The inner character of a person
is the true measure of lasting greatness.
BILLY GRAHAM

Character is built over a lifetime.
ELIZABETH GEORGE

Remember that your character
is the sum total of your habits.
RICK WARREN

More from God's Word

Whoever walks in integrity walks securely,
but whoever takes crooked paths will be found out.
PROVERBS 10:9 NIV

The godly walk with integrity;
blessed are their children after them.
PROVERBS 20:7 NLT

The integrity of the upright guides them,
but the perversity of the treacherous destroys them.
PROVERBS 11:3 HCSB

He stores up success for the upright;
He is a shield for those who live with integrity.
PROVERBS 2:7 HCSB

Let integrity and uprightness preserve me,
for I wait for You.
PSALM 25:21 NKJV

A Timely Tip

Some people encourage you to do things that you know to be wrong. People who want you to betray your conscience are dangerous to your physical, mental, and spiritual health. So your best strategy is to actively avoid people who want you to compromise yourself. Life is too short to bear the weight of a guilty conscience.

18

CHEERFULNESS

CHEERFULNESS: IT'S GOOD MEDICINE

A cheerful heart is good medicine,
but a crushed spirit dries up the bones.
PROVERBS 17:22 NIV

When you encounter someone whose behavior is unfriendly, unhelpful, dishonest, or inappropriate, you'll be tempted to lose your temper. If so, you are not alone. Even the most righteous among us are beset by fits of ill temper and frustration. During these moments, we may not feel like turning our thoughts and prayers to Christ, but that's precisely what we should do.

English clergyman Charles Kingsley observed, "The people whom I have seen succeed best in life have always been cheerful and hopeful people who went about their business with smiles on their faces" And John Wesley noted, "Sour godliness is the devil's religion." These words remind us that pessimism and doubt are some of the most important tools that Satan uses to achieve his objectives. Our challenge, of course, is to ensure that Satan cannot use these tools on us.

Are you a cheerful Christian even when times are tough and people are being difficult? You should be! And what is the best way to attain the joy that is rightfully yours? By giving Christ what is rightfully His: your heart, your soul, and your life.

MORE THOUGHTS ABOUT CHEERFULNESS

It is not fitting, when one is in God's service, to have a gloomy face or a chilling look.
ST. FRANCIS OF ASSISI

The practical effect of Christianity is happiness, therefore let it be spread abroad everywhere!
C. H. SPURGEON

A life of intimacy with God is characterized by joy.
OSWALD CHAMBERS

The greatest honor you can give Almighty God is to live gladly and joyfully because of the knowledge of His love.
JULIANA OF NORWICH

God is good, and heaven is forever. And if those two facts don't cheer you up, nothing will.
MARIE T. FREEMAN

More from God's Word

A cheerful heart has a continual feast.
PROVERBS 15:15 HCSB

Shout for joy to the LORD, all the earth.
Worship the LORD with gladness;
come before him with joyful songs.
PSALM 100:1–2 NIV

Rejoice always, pray without ceasing,
in everything give thanks;
for this is the will of God in Christ Jesus for you.
1 THESSALONIANS 5:16–18 NKJV

This is the day that the LORD has made.
Let us rejoice and be glad today!
PSALM 118:24 NCV

Do everything without grumbling and arguing,
so that you may be blameless and pure.
PHILIPPIANS 2:14–15 HCSB

A Timely Tip

Cheerfulness is its own reward, but not its only reward. When you sow a positive attitude, you'll reap a positive life.

19

CHRIST'S LOVE

EXPERIENCING CHRIST'S LOVE AND SHARING IT

We love him, because he first loved us.
1 JOHN 4:19 KJV

Hannah Whitall Smith spoke to believers of every generation when she advised, "Keep your face upturned to Christ as the flowers do to the sun. Look, and your soul shall live and grow." But when we're dealing with difficult people, it becomes harder to focus on Christ's love because we are overwhelmed by other emotions. It's hard to focus on Jesus, but not impossible. When we turn our hearts to Him we receive His blessings, His peace, and His grace.

Christ is the ultimate Savior of mankind and the personal savior of those who believe in Him. As His servants, we should place Him at the very center of our lives. And every day that God gives us breath, we should share Christ's love and His message with a world that needs both.

Christ's love changes everything, including you. When you accept His gift of grace, you are transformed, not only for the moment, but also for all eternity. He's waiting patiently for you to invite Him into your heart. Please don't make Him wait a single minute longer.

More Thoughts about Christ's Love

Above all else, the Christian life
is a love affair of the heart.
John Eldredge

Jesus: the proof of God's love.
Phillip Yancey

Jesus is all compassion.
He never betrays us.
Catherine Marshall

As the love of a husband for his bride,
such is the love of Christ for His people.
C. H. Spurgeon

The love of God exists in its strongest
and purest form in the very midst
of suffering and tragedy.
Suzanne Dale Ezell

MORE FROM GOD'S WORD

As the Father loved Me,
I also have loved you; abide in My love.
JOHN 15:9 NKJV

For Christ also suffered once for sins, the just for the unjust,
that He might bring us to God, being put to death
in the flesh but made alive by the Spirit.
1 PETER 3:18 NKJV

I am the good shepherd. The good shepherd
lays down his life for the sheep.
JOHN 10:11 HCSB

No one has greater love than this,
that someone would lay down his life for his friends.
JOHN 15:13 HCSB

For God so loved the world,
that he gave his only begotten Son,
that whosoever believeth in him should not perish,
but have everlasting life.
JOHN 3:16 KJV

A TIMELY TIP

Christ's love is meant to be experienced—and shared—by you. And our Lord wants you to share His love with all people, not just the ones with easygoing personalities.

20

CHURCH

WHEN PEOPLE ARE
DIFFICULT IN CHURCH

*Be on guard for yourselves and for all the flock that
the Holy Spirit has appointed you to as overseers, to shepherd
the church of God, which He purchased with His own blood.*
ACTS 20:28 HCSB

From time to time, you may encounter difficult people at church.
You should not be surprised by this fact, and you shouldn't let
someone else's prickly personality discourage you from attending
worship services.

Regular church attendance builds the spiritual muscle and
the emotional strength that you need to deal with difficult people,
problematic relationships, and unfortunate circumstances. So don't
let other people's misbehavior dissuade you from attending church.
Instead, go to church with a smile on your face and love in your
heart. When you do, you'll be blessed by the vast majority of men
and women who attend your fellowship, *and* you'll be blessed by
your Creator.

You deserve to attend church, and God deserves for you to
attend church, so act—and worship—accordingly.

More Thoughts about Church

Every believer is commanded
to be plugged in to a local church.
David Jeremiah

The church is a hospital for sinners,
not a museum for saints.
Vance Havner

Churchgoers are like coals in a fire.
When they cling together,
they keep the flame aglow;
when they separate, they die out.
Billy Graham

The Church will outlive the universe;
in it the individual person will outlive the universe.
C. S. Lewis

Divisions between Christians
are a sin and a scandal,
and Christians ought at all times
to be making contributions toward reunion,
if it is only by their prayers.
C. S. Lewis

More from God's Word

I was glad when they said unto me,
Let us go into the house of the LORD.
PSALM 122:1 KJV

God is spirit, and those who worship Him
must worship in spirit and truth.
JOHN 4:24 HCSB

For where two or three gather in my name,
there am I with them.
MATTHEW 18:20 NIV

Enter his gates with thanksgiving; go into his courts
with praise. Give thanks to him and bless his name.
PSALM 100:4 NLT

Worship the Lord your God and...serve Him only.
MATTHEW 4:10 HCSB

A Timely Tip

When your brothers and sisters in the church are being difficult, don't take it personally and stop attending services. We humans are imperfect and our problems are temporary; God's church is eternal, and so are His rewards.

21

COMMUNICATION SKILLS

WATCH YOUR WORDS

If anyone thinks he is religious without controlling his tongue, then his religion is useless and he deceives himself.
JAMES 1:26 HCSB

In the book of Proverbs, we are taught time and again that the words we speak can and should be beautiful offerings to those who hear them. But we are also warned that our words can have unhappy consequences when we speak impulsively, thoughtlessly, or angrily. Of course, it's especially hard to control our words when we're reacting to a person who's behaving badly. But God's Word tells us that we should always measure our words carefully before we speak them, especially in emotionally charged situations.

Sometimes even the most thoughtful among us speak first and think second (with decidedly mixed results). When we're dealing with difficult people, we may speak words that would be better left unspoken. Yet whenever we lash out in anger, we forgo the wonderful opportunity to consider our thoughts before we give voice to them.

A far better strategy, of course, is to do the more difficult thing: to think first and to speak next. When we do so, we give ourselves ample time to compose our thoughts and to consult our Creator (but not necessarily in that order!).

The Bible warns us that we will be judged by the words we speak (Matthew 12:36–37). And Ephesians 4:29 reminds us that we can—and should—make "each word a gift" (MSG). To do otherwise is to invite God's displeasure. Do you seek to be a source of encouragement to everybody, including the people who possess prickly personalities? And do you seek to be a worthy ambassador for Christ? If so, you must speak words that are worthy of God's Son. So avoid angry outbursts. Refrain from impulsive outpourings. Terminate tantrums. Instead, speak words of encouragement and hope to a world that desperately needs both. Do you always measure your words carefully, even when you're tempted to unleash a verbal barrage? If so, you are both wise and blessed. But if you're like most people, you may, on occasion, speak before you think and then have reason to regret the things you've said.

Today, take control of your words by engaging your mind *before* you rev up your vocal cords. After all, some things are better left unsaid, and you never have to apologize for the words you *didn't* speak.

MORE THOUGHTS ABOUT WATCHING YOUR WORDS

Better to slip with foot than tongue.
BEN FRANKLIN

Words. Do you fully understand their power?
Can any of us really grasp the mighty force
behind the things we say? Do we stop
and think before we speak,
considering the potency of the words we utter?
JONI EARECKSON TADA

The great test of a man's character is his tongue.
OSWALD CHAMBERS

If you are to be self-controlled
in your speech you must be
self-controlled in your thinking.
FRANÇOIS FÈNELON

When you talk, choose the very same words
that you would use if Jesus
were looking over your shoulder. Because He is.
MARIE T. FREEMAN

More from God's Word

A word fitly spoken is like apples of gold in settings of silver.
PROVERBS 25:11 NKJV

What you have said in the dark
will be heard in the light,
and what you have whispered in an inner room
will be shouted from the housetops.
LUKE 12:3 NCV

The heart of the wise teaches his mouth,
and adds learning to his lips.
PROVERBS 16:23 NKJV

Pleasant words are a honeycomb:
sweet to the taste and health to the body.
PROVERBS 16:24 HCSB

But encourage each other daily,
while it is still called today,
so that none of you is hardened by sin's deception.
HEBREWS 3:13 HCSB

A Timely Tip

If you're not sure what to say, ask yourself this question: "What would Jesus say if He were here?" Then you'll have the answer.

22

COMPLAINING

COMPLAINING DOESN'T MAKE IT BETTER

Be hospitable to one another without complaining.
1 PETER 4:9 HCSB

When we find ourselves dealing with difficult people, it's easy to become frustrated, and it's easy to complain. So in our weakest moments we're tempted to grumble, to whine, and to moan about difficult people or the difficult circumstances they seem to create on a daily basis. Sometimes we give voice to our complaints, and on other occasions we manage to keep our protestations to ourselves. But even when no one else hears our complaints, God does.

Would you like to feel more comfortable about your circumstances and your life? Then promise yourself that you'll do whatever it takes to ensure that you focus your thoughts and energy on the major blessings you've received, not the minor hardships—or the difficult people—you must occasionally endure.

So the next time you're tempted to complain about the inevitable frustrations of everyday living, don't do it. Today and every day, make it a practice to count your blessings, not your inconveniences. It's the truly decent way to live.

More Thoughts
about Complaining

*Whenever you catch yourself starting
to complain about someone, you would do well
to turn your thoughts inward
and inspect your own thoughts and deeds.*
St. Stephen of Muret

*It is always possible to be thankful for what
is given rather than to complain about what is not given.
One or the other becomes a habit of life.*
Elisabeth Elliot

*Thanksgiving or complaining—these words express
two contrasting attitudes of the souls of God's children.
The soul that gives thanks can find comfort in everything;
the soul that complains can find comfort in nothing.*
Hannah Whitall Smith

*Don't complain. The more you complain about things,
the more things you'll have to complain about.*
E. Stanley Jones

*Grumbling and gratitude are,
for the child of God, in conflict.
Be grateful and you won't grumble.
Grumble and you won't be grateful.*
Billy Graham

More from God's Word

Do everything without complaining or arguing.
Then you will be innocent and without any wrong.
PHILIPPIANS 2:14–15 NCV

Those who consider themselves religious
and yet do not keep a tight rein on their tongues
deceive themselves, and their religion is worthless.
JAMES 1:26 NIV

Those who guard their lips preserve their lives,
but those who speak rashly will come to ruin.
PROVERBS 13:3 NIV

A fool's displeasure is known at once,
but whoever ignores an insult is sensible.
PROVERBS 12:16 HCSB

My dear brothers and sisters,
always be willing to listen and slow to speak.
JAMES 1:19 NCV

A Timely Tip

If you feel a personal pity party coming on, slow down and start counting your blessings. If you fill your heart with gratitude, there's simply no room left for complaints.

23

CONSCIENCE

KEEP YOUR CONSCIENCE CLEAR

*So I strive always to keep my
conscience clear before God and man.*
ACTS 24:16 NIV

God has given each of us a conscience, and He intends for us to use it. But sometimes troubled people encourage us to betray our values and rush headlong into situations that we may soon come to regret. When a person with a difficult personality encourages you to stray from the path God has set before you, you may be tempted to tune out the quiet inner voice that warns against disobedience and danger. It's a temptation that you must resist if you wish to avoid a string of negative consequences.

God promises that He rewards good conduct and that He blesses those who obey His Word. The Lord also issues a stern warning to those who rebel against His commandments. Wise men and women heed that warning. Count yourself among their number.

Sometime soon, perhaps today, your conscience will speak; when it does, listen carefully. God may be trying to get a message through to you. Don't miss it.

More Thoughts about Trusting Your Conscience

God speaks through a variety of means.
In the present God primarily speaks
by the Holy Spirit, through the Bible,
prayer, circumstances, and the church.

Henry Blackaby

It is neither safe nor prudent
to do anything against conscience.

Martin Luther

The conscience is a built-in
warning system that signals us
when something we have done is wrong.

John MacArthur

Conscience is God's voice to the inner man.

Billy Graham

Conscience can only be satisfied if God is satisfied.

C. H. Spurgeon

More from God's Word

Now the goal of our instruction is love from a pure heart,
a good conscience, and a sincere faith.
1 TIMOTHY 1:5 HCSB

Create in me a clean heart, O God;
and renew a right spirit within me.
PSALM 51:10 KJV

Let us come near to God with a sincere heart
and a sure faith, because we have been made free
from a guilty conscience, and our bodies
have been washed with pure water.
HEBREWS 10:22 NCV

People's thoughts can be like a deep well, but someone
with understanding can find the wisdom there.
PROVERBS 20:5 NCV

Behold, the kingdom of God is within you.
LUKE 17:21 KJV

A Timely Tip

Some folks, especially people with problematic personalities, may encourage you to betray your conscience. Don't do it! When your conscience speaks, listen carefully. When you let your conscience guide you, you'll be safer and happier.

24

COURAGE

WHEN PEOPLE ARE DIFFICULT, HAVE COURAGE

*For God has not given us a spirit of fearfulness,
but one of power, love, and sound judgment.*
2 TIMOTHY 1:7 HCSB

It takes courage to deal with difficult people, and Christians have every reason to live courageously. After all, the ultimate battle has already been fought and won on the cross at Calvary. But even dedicated followers of Christ may find their strength and patience tested when people misbehave.

Every human life is a tapestry woven together by events and relationships. Some of the threads are wonderful, some not so wonderful, and some downright disheartening. When we're forced to deal with a difficult person, the storm clouds may form overhead and we may find ourselves wandering through an emotional valley of anger on one side and hopelessness on the other. During these troubling times, our faith is stretched, sometimes to the breaking point. But as believers, we can be comforted: wherever we find ourselves, whether at the top of the mountain or in the depths of the valley, God is there, and because He cares for us, we can live courageously.

The next time you find yourself in a fear-provoking situation, remember that God is as near as your next breath, and remember that He offers salvation to His children. He is your shield and your strength; He is your protector and your deliverer. Call upon Him in your hour of need and then be comforted. Whatever your challenge, whatever your trouble, God can handle it. And will.

MORE THOUGHTS ABOUT COURAGE

Action springs not from thought,
but from a readiness for responsibility.
DIETRICH BONHOEFFER

Just as courage is faith in good, so discouragement
is faith in evil, and, while courage opens the door to good,
discouragement opens it to evil.
HANNAH WHITALL SMITH

Courage is not simply one of the virtues,
but the form of every virtue at the testing point.
C. S. LEWIS

In my experience, God rarely makes our fear disappear.
Instead, He asks us to be strong and take courage.
BRUCE WILKINSON

Do not limit the limitless God! With Him,
face the future unafraid because you are never alone.
LETTIE COWMAN

More from God's Word

Be strong and courageous, and do the work.
Do not be afraid or discouraged,
for the Lord God, my God, is with you.
1 Chronicles 28:20 NIV

But He said to them,
"It is I; do not be afraid."
John 6:20 NKJV

Be on guard. Stand firm in the faith.
Be courageous. Be strong.
1 Corinthians 16:13 NLT

I can do all things through Him who strengthens me.
Philippians 4:13 NASB

Behold, God is my salvation;
I will trust, and not be afraid.
Isaiah 12:2 KJV

A Timely Tip

It takes insight and courage to deal effectively with difficult people and difficult circumstances. If you need insight, talk to folks you trust and spend time studying God's Word. And if you need courage, ask the Lord to help you do what needs to be done. Now.

25

COURTESY

EVEN WHEN PEOPLE ARE DIFFICULT, COURTESY COUNTS

Finally, all of you be of one mind, having compassion for one another; love as brothers, be tenderhearted, be courteous.

1 PETER 3:8 NKJV

When you encounter someone who is discourteous, you're tempted to respond in kind, perhaps with an angry outburst or cruel word. Your challenge, as a Christian, is to resist that temptation.

Here in the twenty-first century, it sometimes seems like common courtesy is a decidedly uncommon trait. But if we are to trust the Bible—and we should—then we should understand that kindness and courtesy will never go out of style.

God's Word makes it clear that we should treat others as we ourselves wish to be treated (Matthew 7:12). That means that we must be courteous to others, even when it's hard.

Today try to be a little kinder than necessary to everyone, even the difficult people. And as you consider all the things God has done for you, honor Him with your good deeds and kind words. The Lord deserves your best, and you deserve the experience of giving it to Him.

More Thoughts about Courtesy

Every time you smile at someone,
it is an action of love,
a gift to that person, a beautiful thing.
MOTHER TERESA

Hospitality is threefold:
for one's family, this of necessity; for strangers,
this is courtesy; for the poor, this is charity.
THOMAS FULLER

Courtesy is contagious.
OLD SAYING

The glory of the home is hospitality.
HENRY VAN DYKE

The Golden Rule starts at home,
but it should never stop there.
MARIE T. FREEMAN

More from God's Word

Let everyone see that you are gentle and kind.
The Lord is coming soon.
Philippians 4:5 NCV

Kind words are like honey—
sweet to the soul and healthy for the body.
Proverbs 16:24 NLT

So, my friends, when you come together to the Lord's Table,
be reverent and courteous with one another.
1 Corinthians 11:33 MSG

Do to others as you would have them do to you.
Luke 6:31 NIV

Do not neglect to show hospitality to strangers,
for by this some have entertained angels without knowing it.
Hebrews 13:2 NASB

A Timely Tip

When people are discourteous to you, you don't have to respond in kind. The Golden Rule applies, even when people behave badly. So don't feel compelled to fight fire with fire. Instead, be as courteous as you can and keep your temper in check. Remember that anger is only one letter away from danger.

26

DAILY DEVOTIONAL

START EVERY DAY WITH GOD

Morning by morning he wakens me and opens
my understanding to his will. The Sovereign LORD
has spoken to me, and I have listened.

ISAIAH 50:4–5 NLT

A great way to prepare yourself for the rigors of everyday living is by spending a few moments with God every morning. Whether you're dealing with difficult people or stressful circumstances or both, you need God as your partner. So if you find that you're simply "too busy" for a daily chat with your Father in heaven, it's time to take a long, hard look at your priorities and your values.

Each day has 1,440 minutes. Do you value your relationship with God enough to spend a few of those minutes with Him? He deserves that much of your time and more. Is He receiving it from you? Hopefully so.

As you consider your plans for the day ahead, here's a tip: organize your life around this simple principle: God first. When you place your Creator where He belongs—at the very center of your day and your life—the rest of your priorities will fall into place.

More Thoughts about Your Daily Devotional

Whatever is your best time in the day,
give that to communion with God.
Hudson Taylor

Relying on God has to begin
all over again every day
as if nothing had yet been done.
C. S. Lewis

Make it the first morning business of your life
to understand some part of the Bible clearly,
and make it your daily business to obey it.
John Ruskin

Begin each day with God.
It will change your priorities.
Elizabeth George

Doesn't God deserve the best minutes of your day?
Billy Graham

More from God's Word

It is good to give thanks to the LORD,
and to sing praises to Your name, O Most High.
PSALM 92:1 NKJV

Early the next morning, while it was still dark,
Jesus woke and left the house.
He went to a lonely place, where he prayed.
MARK 1:35 NCV

Heaven and earth will pass away,
but My words will never pass away.
MATTHEW 24:35 HCSB

Thy word is a lamp unto my feet,
and a light unto my path.
PSALM 119:105 KJV

But grow in the grace and knowledge
of our Lord and Savior Jesus Christ.
To Him be the glory both now and to the day of eternity.
2 PETER 3:18 HCSB

A Timely Tip

A regular time of quiet reflection, prayer, and Bible study will allow you to praise your Creator, to focus your thoughts, and to seek God's guidance on matters great and small. Don't miss this opportunity.

27

DEPRESSION

UNDERSTANDING DEPRESSION

He heals the brokenhearted and binds up their wounds.
PSALM 147:3 HCSB

If a difficult person has put you in a stressful situation with no end in sight, you may become depressed. If so, it's important to understand that depression is an illness, not a weakness or a sin.

Clinical depression is a serious, life-threatening condition, and you should treat it that way. The sooner you seek treatment, the sooner you'll begin to feel better. The longer you avoid treatment, the longer you'll suffer.

So if you're feeling depressed—or if someone you care about appears to be feeling that way—don't hesitate to call your doctor, who can rule out other causes for your distress and, if needed, make a referral to a physician who specializes in mental illnesses.

Mental illness is nothing to be ashamed of, and help is readily available. So trust God and trust your doctors. Keep praying; keep reading your Bible; and keep the faith. And while you're at it, keep in close contact with medical professionals, who, by the way, know more about treating clinical depression than you do.

More Thoughts about Depression

*Perhaps the greatest psychological, spiritual,
and medical need that all people have is the need for hope.*
BILLY GRAHAM

*Feelings of uselessness and hopelessness
are not from God, but from the evil one,
the devil, who wants to discourage you
and thwart your effectiveness for the Lord.*
BILL BRIGHT

*I am sure it is never sadness—
a proper, straight, natural response to loss—
that does people harm, but all the other things,
all the resentment, dismay, doubt,
and self-pity with which it is usually complicated.*
C. S. LEWIS

*Emotions we have not poured out
in the safe hands of God can turn into feelings
of hopelessness and depression. God is safe.*
BETH MOORE

*What the devil loves is that vague cloud
of unspecified guilt feeling or unspecified virtue
by which he lures us into despair or presumption.*
C. S. LEWIS

More from God's Word

Why are you cast down, O my soul? And why are you disquieted within me? Hope in God; for I shall yet praise Him, the help of my countenance and my God.
PSALM 42:11 NKJV

Weeping may endure for a night, but joy comes in the morning.
PSALM 30:5 NKJV

When I sit in darkness, the LORD will be a light to me.
MICAH 7:8 NKJV

Blessed are the poor in spirit: for theirs is the kingdom of heaven. Blessed are they that mourn: for they shall be comforted.
MATTHEW 5:3-4 KJV

Your heart must not be troubled. Believe in God; believe also in Me.
JOHN 14:1 HCSB

A Timely Tip

If you're feeling very sad or deeply depressed, talk about it with people who can help. Don't hesitate to speak with your doctor or your pastor or both. Help is available. Ask for it now.

28

DIFFICULT CIRCUMSTANCES

TRUST HIM IN EVERY CIRCUMSTANCE

Trust in him at all times, you people;
pour out your hearts to him, for God is our refuge.
PSALM 62:8 NIV

You've probably heard it said on many occasions. Perhaps you've even said it yourself: "I'm doing the best I can under the circumstances." But God has a better way. He wants you to live *above* your circumstances— and with His help, you can most certainly do it.

In the fourth chapter of Philippians, Paul stated that he could find happiness and fulfillment in any situation. How? By turning his life and his future over to God. Even when he faced enormous difficulties, Paul found peace through God. So can you.

Today, make this important promise to yourself and to your Creator: Promise to rise far above your circumstances. You deserve no less...and neither, for that matter, does your Father in heaven.

More Thoughts about Trusting God in Difficult Circumstances

Jesus did not promise to change
the circumstances around us.
He promised great peace and pure joy
to those who would learn to believe
that God actually controls all things.

Corrie ten Boom

Every experience God gives us,
every person He brings into our lives,
is the perfect preparation
for the future that only He can see.

Corrie ten Boom

Don't let obstacles along
the road to eternity shake your
confidence in God's promises.

David Jeremiah

Accept each day as it comes to you.
Do not waste your time and energy
wishing for a different set of circumstances.

Sarah Young

No matter what our circumstance,
we can find a reason to be thankful.

David Jeremiah

More from God's Word

The LORD is a refuge for
His people and a stronghold.
JOEL 3:16 NASB

God is our protection and our strength.
He always helps in times of trouble.
PSALM 46:1 NCV

The LORD is a refuge for the oppressed,
a refuge in times of trouble.
PSALM 9:9 HCSB

Cast your burden on the LORD,
and He shall sustain you;
He shall never permit the righteous to be moved.
PSALM 55:22 NKJV

I have learned in whatever state I am, to be content.
PHILIPPIANS 4:11 NKJV

A Timely Tip

No circumstances are too tough for God, and no problems are too big for Him. When times are tough, cast your burden upon Him, and He will sustain you.

29

DIFFICULT PEOPLE

WHEN SOMEONE IS
BEING DIFFICULT, STAY CALM

Bad temper is contagious—don't get infected.
PROVERBS 22:25 MSG

Sometimes people can be cruel, discourteous, untruthful, or rude. When other people do or say things that are hurtful, you may be tempted to strike back with a verbal salvo of your own. But before you say words that can never be unsaid, slow down, say a quiet prayer, and remember this: God corrects other people's behavior in His own way, and He doesn't need your help (even if you're totally convinced you're in the right).

So, when other people behave cruelly, foolishly, or impulsively—as they will from time to time—don't allow yourself to become caught up in their emotional distress. Instead, speak up for yourself as politely as you can and, if necessary, walk away. Next, forgive everybody as quickly as you can. Then get on with your life, and leave the rest up to God.

More Thoughts about Difficult People

How often should you forgive the other person?
Only as many times as you want God to forgive you!
Marie T. Freeman

If you are a Christian,
you are not a citizen of this world
trying to get to heaven;
you are a citizen of heaven
making your way through this world.
Vance Havner

We are all fallen creatures
and all very hard to live with.
C. S. Lewis

Give me such love for God and men
as will blot out all hatred and bitterness.
Dietrich Bonhoeffer

Whatever a person may be like,
we must still love them because we love God.
John Calvin

MORE FROM GOD'S WORD

A perverse man stirs up conflict,
and a gossip separates close friends.
PROVERBS 16:28 NIV

Don't make friends with an angry man,
and don't be a companion of a hot-tempered man,
or you will learn his ways and entangle yourself in a snare.
PROVERBS 22:24–25 HCSB

Stay away from a foolish man;
you will gain no knowledge from his speech.
PROVERBS 14:7 HCSB

A person with great anger bears the penalty;
if you rescue him, you'll have to do it again.
PROVERBS 19:19 HCSB

Mockers can get a whole town agitated,
but those who are wise will calm anger.
PROVERBS 29:8 NLT

A TIMELY TIP

Sometimes misguided people attempt to alleviate their own pain by inflicting pain upon others. If you find yourself on the receiving end of someone else's wrath, give yourself permission to walk away from that painful encounter.

30

DIFFICULT RELATIONSHIPS

SOME RELATIONSHIPS ARE
DANGEROUS TO YOUR MENTAL HEALTH

*It is safer to meet a bear robbed of her cubs
than to confront a fool caught in foolishness.*
PROVERBS 17:12 NLT

Emotional health is contagious, and so is emotional distress.
If you're fortunate enough to be surrounded by family members
and friends who celebrate life and praise God, consider yourself
profoundly blessed. But if you find yourself caught in an unhealthy
relationship, it's time to look realistically at your situation and
begin making changes.

Don't worry about changing other people: you can't do it. What
you can do is conduct yourself in a responsible fashion and insist
that other people treat you with the dignity and consideration that
you deserve.

In a perfect world filled with perfect people, our relationships,
too, would be perfect. But none of us are perfect and neither are our
relationships...and that's okay. As we work to make our imperfect
relationships a little happier and healthier, we grow as individuals
and as families. But if we find ourselves in relationships that are

debilitating or dangerous, then changes must be made, and soon.

If you find yourself caught up in a personal relationship that is bringing havoc into your life, and if you can't seem to find the courage to do something about it, don't hesitate to consult your pastor. Or you may choose to seek the advice of a trusted friend or a professionally trained counselor. But whatever you do, don't be satisfied with the status quo.

God has grand plans for your life; He has promised you the joy and abundance that can be yours through Him. But to fully experience God's gifts, you need happy, emotionally healthy people to share them with. It's up to you to make sure that you do your part to build the kinds of relationships that will bring abundance to you, to your family, and to God's world.

MORE THOUGHTS ABOUT DIFFICULT RELATIONSHIPS

We never get anywhere—nor do our conditions and circumstances change—when we look at the dark side of life.
LETTIE COWMAN

Feelings of uselessness and hopelessness are not from God, but from the evil one, the devil, who wants to discourage you and thwart your effectiveness for the Lord.
BILL BRIGHT

If your hopes are being disappointed just now, it means that they are being purified.
OSWALD CHAMBERS

*If I am asked how we are to get rid of discouragements,
I can only say, as I have had to say of so many other
wrong spiritual habits, we must give them up.*

HANNAH WHITALL SMITH

MORE FROM GOD'S WORD

*Give your burdens to the LORD, and he will take care of you.
He will not permit the godly to slip and fall.*

PSALM 55:22 NLT

God shall wipe away all tears from their eyes.

REVELATION 7:17 KJV

The LORD is a refuge for His people and a stronghold.

JOEL 3:16 NASB

The LORD is near to those who have a broken heart.

PSALM 34:18 NKJV

If God is for us, who is against us?

ROMANS 8:31 HCSB

A TIMELY TIP

If you're having trouble dealing with a difficult person, don't be
discouraged and don't give up hope. There's always something you
can do to make your life better, even if it means breaking off the
relationship. Tough times never last, but determined, optimistic,
faith-filled people do.

31

DISAPPOINTMENTS

WHEN YOU'RE DISAPPOINTED, HE CAN HEAL YOUR HEART

*Then they cried out to the LORD in their trouble,
and He saved them out of their distresses.*
PSALM 107:13 NKJV

As we deal with difficult people—as we will from time to time—disappointments and frustrations are inevitable. No matter how competent we are, no matter how hard we try, we still encounter relationships that fall far short of our expectations. When we're disappointed, we have choices to make: we can feel sorry for ourselves or we can get angry or we can become depressed. Or we can get busy praying about our problems and solving them.

When we are disheartened—on those cloudy days when our strength is sapped and our hope is shaken—there exists a source from which we can draw perspective and courage. That source is God. When we turn everything over to Him, we find that He is sufficient to meet our needs. No problem is too big for Him.

So the next time you feel discouraged, slow down long enough to have a serious talk with your Creator. Pray for guidance, pray for strength, and pray for the wisdom to trust your heavenly Father. Your troubles are temporary; His love is not.

MORE THOUGHTS ABOUT DEALING WITH DISAPPOINTMENTS

Let God enlarge you when you are going through distress. He can do it.
WARREN WIERSBE

Unless we learn to deal with disappointment, it will rob us of joy and poison our souls.
BILLY GRAHAM

We all have sorrows and disappointments, but one must never forget that, if commended to God, they will issue in good. His own solution is far better than any we could conceive.
FANNY CROSBY

If your hopes are being disappointed just now, it means that they are being purified.
OSWALD CHAMBERS

Discouragement is the opposite of faith. It is Satan's device to thwart the work of God in your life.
BILLY GRAHAM

More from God's Word

He heals the brokenhearted
and binds up their wounds.
PSALM 147:3 HCSB

My son, do not despise the chastening
of the Lord, nor be discouraged
when you are rebuked by Him.
HEBREWS 12:5 NKJV

He shall not be afraid of evil tidings:
his heart is fixed, trusting in the LORD.
PSALM 112:7 KJV

Many adversities come to the one
who is righteous, but the LORD
delivers him from them all.
PSALM 34:19 HCSB

They that sow in tears shall reap in joy.
PSALM 126:5 KJV

A Timely Tip

When you're discouraged, disappointed, or hurt, don't spend too much time asking, "Why me, Lord?" Instead ask, "What now, Lord?" and then get busy. When you do, you'll feel much better.

32

EMOTIONS

LEARNING TO DEAL EFFECTIVELY WITH YOUR EMOTIONS

Grow a wise heart—you'll do yourself a favor;
keep a clear head—you'll find a good life.
PROVERBS 19:8 MSG

Time and again, the Bible instructs us to live by faith. Yet, despite our best intentions, difficult people and the negative feelings they engender can rob us of the peace and abundance that could be ours—and should be ours—through Christ. When anger, frustration, impatience, or anxiety separate us from the spiritual blessings that God has in store, we must rethink our priorities. And we must place faith above feelings.

Human emotions are highly variable, decidedly unpredictable, and often unreliable. Our emotions change like the weather, but they're less predictable and far more fickle. So we must learn to live by faith, not by the ups and downs of our own emotional roller coasters.

Who's pulling your emotional strings? Are you allowing highly emotional people or highly charged situations to dictate your moods, or are you wiser than that?

Sometime during the coming day, you may encounter a tough

situation or a difficult person. And as a result, you may be gripped by a strong negative emotion. Distrust it. Rein it in. Test it. And turn it over to God.

Your emotions will inevitably change; God will not. So trust Him completely. When you do, you'll be surprised at how quickly those negative feelings can evaporate into thin air.

MORE THOUGHTS ABOUT CONTROLLING YOUR EMOTIONS

If you desire to improve your physical well-being and your emotional outlook, increasing your faith can help you.
JOHN MAXWELL

A life lived in God is not lived on the plane of feelings, but of the will.
ELISABETH ELLIOT

Our feelings do not affect God's facts.
AMY CARMICHAEL

Our emotions can lie to us, and we need to counter our emotions with truth.
BILLY GRAHAM

It is Christ who is to be exalted, not our feelings. We will know Him by obedience, not by emotions. Our love will be shown by obedience, not by how good we feel about God at a given moment.
ELISABETH ELLIOT

More from God's Word

*For this very reason, make every effort to supplement
your faith with goodness, goodness with knowledge,
knowledge with self-control, self-control
with endurance, endurance with godliness.*
2 PETER 1:5–6 HCSB

*Get wisdom—how much better it is than gold!
And get understanding—it is preferable to silver.*
PROVERBS 16:16 HCSB

*And let the peace of God rule in your hearts,
to which also you were called in one body; and be thankful.*
COLOSSIANS 3:15 NKJV

*All bitterness, anger and wrath, shouting and slander must
be removed from you, along with all malice.
And be kind and compassionate to one another, forgiving
one another, just as God also forgave you in Christ.*
EPHESIANS 4:31–32 HCSB

A Timely Tip

Are you sometimes overly emotional? If so, here are the facts: God's love is real; His peace is real; His support is real. Don't ever let your emotions obscure these facts. And when you encounter difficult people, and you will, say a silent prayer and let God handle the things you can't.

33

ENTHUSIASM

KEEP YOUR ENTHUSIASM UP

*Whatever you do, do it enthusiastically,
as something done for the Lord and not for men.*
COLOSSIANS 3:23 HCSB

Difficult people have a way of sapping your enthusiasm and stealing your joy. When you encounter someone like that, your task is to avoid the emotional quicksand and remain positive. Maintaining your composure can be a difficult task, but with God as your partner, you can do it.

Do you see each day as a glorious opportunity to serve God and to do His will? Are you enthused about life, or do you struggle through each day giving scarcely a thought to God's blessings? Are you constantly praising God for His gifts, and are you sharing His Good News with the world? And are you excited about the possibilities for service that God has placed before you, whether at home, at work, at church, or at school? You should be.

You are the recipient of Christ's sacrificial love. Accept it enthusiastically and share it fervently, even when you find yourself in difficult situations. Jesus deserves your enthusiasm; the world deserves it; and you deserve the experience of sharing it.

More Thoughts about Enthusiasm

Two types of voices command your attention today.
Negative ones fill your mind with doubt, bitterness, and fear.
Positive ones purvey hope and strength.
Which one will you choose to heed?
Max Lucado

Developing a positive attitude
means working continually to find
what is uplifting and encouraging.
Barbara Johnson

Wherever you are, be all there.
Live to the hilt every situation
you believe to be the will of God.
Jim Elliot

Those who have achieved excellence in the practice
of an art or profession have commonly been motivated
by great enthusiasm in their pursuit of it.
John Knox

We act as though comfort and luxury were the chief
requirements of life, when all that we need to make us really
happy is something to be enthusiastic about.
Charles Kingsley

More from God's Word

Do your work with enthusiasm. Work as if you were serving the Lord, not as if you were serving only men and women.
Ephesians 6:7 NCV

Rejoice always! Pray constantly. Give thanks in everything, for this is God's will for you in Christ Jesus.
1 Thessalonians 5:16–18 HCSB

A happy heart makes the face cheerful, but heartache crushes the spirit.
Proverbs 15:13 NIV

But as for me, I will hope continually, and will praise You yet more and more.
Psalm 71:14 NASB

Let the hearts of those who seek the Lord rejoice. Look to the Lord and his strength; seek his face always.
1 Chronicles 16:10–11 NIV

A Timely Tip

People with difficult personalities can make you feel discouraged, or worse. Your challenge is to maintain your enthusiasm for life, even when times are tough. So ask God to help you focus on His blessings. And don't let anybody steal your joy.

34

ENVY

BEYOND ENVY

Let us not be desirous of vain glory,
provoking one another, envying one another.
GALATIANS 5:26 KJV

Some people have the unfortunate habit of flaunting their good fortune. When they do so, we may find ourselves overtaken by a destructive emotion: envy. Envy is emotional poison. It poisons the mind and hardens the heart.

If we are to experience the abundant lives that Christ has promised, we must be on guard against envious thoughts. Jealousy breeds discontent, discontent breeds unhappiness, and unhappiness robs us of the peace that might otherwise be ours.

So if the sin of envy has invaded your heart, ask God to help you heal. When you ask sincerely and often, He will respond. And when He does, you'll regain the peace that can only be found through Him.

More Thoughts about Envy

How can you feel the miseries of envy
when you possess in Christ the best of all portions?
C. H. Spurgeon

Envy shoots at others and wounds herself.
Thomas Fuller

Envy takes the joy, happiness,
and contentment out of living.
Billy Graham

Envy and greed always—
always—exact a terrible price.
Billy Graham

Resentment always hurts you more
than the person you resent.
Rick Warren

More from God's Word

So rid yourselves of all malice, all deceit,
hypocrisy, envy, and all slander.
1 PETER 2:1 HCSB

Where jealousy and selfishness are,
there will be confusion and every kind of evil.
JAMES 3:16 NCV

You must not covet your neighbor's house.
You must not covet your neighbor's wife
male or female servant, ox or donkey,
or anything else your neighbor owns.
EXODUS 20:17 NLT

Let us not become boastful,
challenging one another,
envying one another.
GALATIANS 5:26 NASB

Don't envy evil men or desire to be with them.
PROVERBS 24:1 HCSB

A Timely Tip

You can be envious, or you can be happy, but you can't be both.
Envy and happiness can't live at the same time in the same brain.

35

FAILURE

WHEN THINGS DON'T WORK OUT, DON'T LOSE HOPE

For though the righteous fall seven times, they rise again,
PROVERBS 24:16 NIV

If you're dealing with someone whose personality style is difficult—or worse—you're not going to win every battle, and you're not going to enjoy every encounter. But even when you're faced with bitter disappointments or surprising setbacks, you must never lose faith.

Hebrews 10:36 advises, "Patient endurance is what you need now, so that you will continue to do God's will. Then you will receive all that he has promised" (NLT). These words remind us that when we persevere, we will eventually receive the rewards that God has promised us. What's required is perseverance, not perfection.

When we face difficult relationships or unfortunate circumstances, God stands ready to protect us. Our responsibility, of course, is to ask Him for protection. When we call upon Him in heartfelt prayer, He will answer—in His own time and according to His own plan—and He will do His part to heal us. We, of course, must do our part too. And while we are waiting for God's plans to unfold and for His healing touch to restore us, we can be comforted in the knowledge that our Creator can overcome any obstacle, even if we cannot.

More Thoughts about Failure

Mistakes offer the possibility for redemption
and a new start in God's kingdom. No matter
what you're guilty of, God can restore your innocence.
Barbara Johnson

Failure is one of life's most powerful teachers.
How we handle our failures determines whether we're
going to simply "get by" in life or "press on."
Beth Moore

No matter how badly we have failed,
we can always get up and begin again.
Our God is the God of new beginnings.
Warren Wiersbe

No amount of falls will really undo
us if we keep picking ourselves up after each one.
C. S. Lewis

Those who have failed miserably
are often the first to see God's formula for success.
Erwin Lutzer

More from God's Word

The Lord is near to those who have a broken heart.
PSALM 34:18 NKJV

But as for you, be strong; don't be discouraged,
for your work has a reward.
2 CHRONICLES 15:7 HCSB

If you listen to correction to improve your life,
you will live among the wise.
PROVERBS 15:31 NCV

We are hard-pressed on every side,
yet not crushed; we are perplexed,
but not in despair.
2 CORINTHIANS 4:8 NKJV

Weeping may endure for a night,
but joy comes in the morning.
PSALM 30:5 NKJV

A Timely Tip

When you're dealing with difficult people, setbacks are inevitable; your response to them is optional. You and the Lord, working together, can always find a way to turn a stumbling block into a stepping stone, so don't give up hope. Better days will arrive, and perhaps sooner than you think.

36

FAITH

YOUR FAITH CAN MAKE YOU WHOLE

*And he said unto her, Daughter, thy faith hath
made thee whole; go in peace, and be whole.*
MARK 5:34 KJV

Every life—including yours—is a series of successes and failures, celebrations and disappointments, joys and sorrows. Every step of the way, through every triumph and tragedy, God will stand by your side and strengthen you *if* you have faith in Him. Jesus taught His disciples that if they had faith, they could move mountains. You can too.

When a suffering woman sought healing by merely touching the hem of His cloak, Jesus replied, "Daughter, be of good comfort; thy faith hath made thee whole" (Matthew 9:22 KJV). The message to believers of every generation is clear: we must live by faith today and every day.

When you place your faith, your trust, indeed your life in the hands of Christ Jesus, you'll be amazed at the marvelous things He can do with you and through you. So strengthen your faith through praise, through worship, through Bible study, and through prayer. And trust God's plans. With Him, all things are possible, and He stands ready to open a world of possibilities to you...*if* you have faith.

More Thoughts about Mountain-Moving Faith

I have learned that faith means trusting in advance
what will only make sense in reverse.
PHILLIP YANCEY

Faith does not concern itself
with the entire journey.
One step is enough.
LETTIE COWMAN

Shout the shout of faith.
Nothing can withstand
the triumphant faith
that links itself to omnipotence.
The secret of all successful living
lies in this shout of faith.
HANNAH WHITALL SMITH

Faith is not merely holding on to God.
It is God holding on to you.
CORRIE TEN BOOM

Faith points us beyond our problems
to the hope we have in Christ.
BILLY GRAHAM

More from God's Word

For truly I say to you, if you have faith
as a mustard seed, you shall say to this mountain,
"Move from here to there," and it will move;
and nothing will be impossible to you.
MATTHEW 17:20 NASB

Blessed are they that have not seen,
and yet have believed.
JOHN 20:29 KJV

Don't be afraid, because I am your God.
I will make you strong and will help you;
I will support you with my right hand that saves you.
ISAIAH 41:10 NCV

Don't be afraid. Only believe.
MARK 5:36 HCSB

All things are possible for the one who believes.
MARK 9:23 NCV

A Timely Tip

Think you're in an impossible situation? Think again. You still have options, and God can still move mountains. Your job is to let Him.

37

FAMILY

WHEN FAMILY MEMBERS
BEHAVE BADLY

*All bitterness, anger and wrath, shouting and slander
must be removed from you, along with all malice.
And be kind and compassionate to one another, forgiving
one another, just as God also forgave you in Christ.*
EPHESIANS 4:31–32 HCSB

No family is perfect, and neither, of course, is yours. When problems occur, as they will from time to time, here are a few things to remember:

1. Put God first in every aspect of your life. And while you're at it, put Him first in every aspect of your family's life too (Joshua 24:15).
2. Choose your words carefully. Harsh words are easy to speak and impossible to retrieve, so think before you speak (Proverbs 12:18).
3. Know what to overlook. Until the day that you become perfect, don't expect others to be (Luke 6:36).
4. Don't interfere with the logical consequences that accompany misbehavior. When you enable someone to

continue misbehaving—whether that person is a child or an adult—you encourage continued misbehavior. So don't accept unacceptable behavior (Hebrews 12:5–6).

5. Don't be afraid to seek help. If you're facing family problems that you just can't seem to solve, don't hesitate to consult your pastor or an experienced counselor (Proverbs 1:5).

6. Don't give up on God. And remember: He will never give up on you or your family (Hebrews 10:23).

In spite of the inevitable challenges of family life, your clan is God's gift to you. That little band of men, women, kids, and babies comprises a treasure on temporary loan from the Father above. As you prayerfully seek God's direction, remember that He has important plans for you and yours. It's up to you to live—and to love—accordingly.

More Thoughts about Your Family

I like to think of my family as a big,
beautiful patchwork quilt—each of us so different
yet stitched together by love and life experiences.
Barbara Johnson

The family circle is the supreme conductor of Christianity.
Henry Drummond

A family is a place where principles are hammered
out and honed on the anvil of everyday living.
Charles Swindoll

MORE FROM GOD'S WORD

Choose for yourselves this day whom you will serve....
But as for me and my house, we will serve the LORD.
JOSHUA 24:15 NKJV

Better a dry crust with peace than
a house full of feasting with strife.
PROVERBS 17:1 HCSB

Every kingdom divided against itself is headed
for destruction, and a house divided against itself falls.
LUKE 11:17 HCSB

But if anyone does not provide for his own,
and especially for those of his household,
he has denied the faith and is worse than an unbeliever.
1 TIMOTHY 5:8 NASB

Their first responsibility is to show godliness at home
and repay their parents by taking care of them.
This is something that pleases God.
1 TIMOTHY 5:4 NLT

A TIMELY TIP

When a family member is plagued with a difficult personality, try not to stay perpetually angry. Instead, forgive as quickly as you can and pray for God's guidance. And remember that you can't change other people's personalities; that's between them and God.

38

FEAR

FEAR NOT. GOD IS BIGGER THAN YOUR DIFFICULTIES

Fear not, for I am with you; be not dismayed,
for I am your God. I will strengthen you,
yes, I will help you, I will uphold you
with My righteous right hand.
ISAIAH 41:10 NKJV

If you feel the need to have a frank conversation with a difficult person, you may be experiencing a common emotion: fear. And as a result of that fear, you may have been procrastinating, hoping that things will improve on their own. Unfortunately, most relationship problems are not self-fixing: when we ignore them, they continue. And sometimes they get worse.

If you're facing a tough conversation with a difficult person, you need courage. And God can supply it.

When a frightening storm rose quickly on the Sea of Galilee, Jesus's disciples were afraid. Because of their limited faith, they feared for their lives. When they turned to Jesus, He calmed the waters and He rebuked His disciples for their lack of faith in Him. On occasion, we, like the disciples, are frightened by the inevitable storms of life. Why are we afraid? Because we, like the disciples, possess imperfect faith.

When we genuinely accept God's promises as absolute truth, when we trust Him with life here on earth and life eternal, we have little to fear. Faith in God is the antidote to worry. Faith in God is the foundation of courage and the source of power. Today, let us trust God more completely and, by doing so, move beyond our fears to a place of abundance, assurance, and peace.

More Thoughts about Facing Your Fears

God shields us from most of the things we fear,
but when He chooses not to shield us,
He unfailingly allots grace in the measure needed.
ELISABETH ELLIOT

It is good to remind ourselves that
the will of God comes from the heart of God
and that we need not be afraid.
WARREN WIERSBE

The presence of fear does not mean
you have no faith. Fear visits everyone.
But make your fear a visitor and not a resident.
MAX LUCADO

A perfect faith would lift us absolutely above fear.
GEORGE MACDONALD

More from God's Word

Peace I leave with you; My peace I give to you;
not as the world gives do I give to you.
Do not let your heart be troubled, nor let it be fearful.
JOHN 14:27 NASB

Even though I walk through the darkest valley,
I will fear no evil, for you are with me;
your rod and your staff, they comfort me.
PSALM 23:4 NIV

But He said to them, "It is I; do not be afraid."
JOHN 6:20 NKJV

The LORD is my light and my salvation—
whom should I fear? The LORD is the stronghold of my life—
of whom should I be afraid?
PSALM 27:1 HCSB

Be not afraid, only believe.
MARK 5:36 KJV

A Timely Tip

Are you feeling anxious or fearful? If so, trust God to handle those problems that are simply too big for you to solve. Entrust the future—your future—to the Lord. The two of you, working together, can accomplish great things for His kingdom.

39

FOLLOWING CHRIST

FOLLOW IN HIS FOOTSTEPS
AS CLOSELY AS YOU CAN

Then He said to them all, "If anyone wants to come with Me,
he must deny himself, take up his cross daily, and follow Me."
LUKE 9:23 HCSB

Each day, as we awaken from sleep, we are confronted with countless opportunities to serve God and to follow in the footsteps of His
Son. When we do, our heavenly Father guides our steps and blesses
our endeavors.

Sometimes we encounter difficult people who leave us feeling
angry and discouraged. During these harsh moments, we may be
tempted to offer responses that are decidedly non-Christian. But
God has different plans for us. He intends that we slow down long
enough to think things through and to follow as closely as we can
in the footsteps of His Son. When we do, He lifts our spirits and
guards our hearts.

Today provides a glorious opportunity to place yourself in the
service of the One who is the Giver of all blessings. May you seek
His will, may you trust His Word, and may you walk carefully and
prayerfully in the footsteps of His Son.

More Thoughts about Following Christ

Christ is not valued at all unless He is valued above all.
St. Augustine

*Be assured, if you walk with Him
and look to Him, and expect help from Him,
He will never fail you.*
George Mueller

*A disciple is a follower of Christ.
That means you take on His priorities as your own.
His agenda becomes your agenda.
His mission becomes your mission.*
Charles Stanley

*The crucial question for each of us is this:
What do you think of Jesus, and do you yet
have a personal acquaintance with Him?*
Hannah Whitall Smith

*Choose Jesus Christ! Deny yourself,
take up the Cross, and follow Him,
for the world must be shown.
The world must see, in us,
a discernible, visible, startling difference.*
Elisabeth Elliot

MORE FROM GOD'S WORD

But whoever keeps His word, truly in him the love of God is perfected. This is how we know we are in Him: the one who says he remains in Him should walk just as He walked.

1 JOHN 2:5-6 HCSB

*Take my yoke upon you, and learn of me;
for I am meek and lowly in heart:
and ye shall find rest unto your souls.
For my yoke is easy, and my burden is light.*

MATTHEW 11:29-30 KJV

*Walk in a manner worthy of the God
who calls you into His own kingdom and glory.*

1 THESSALONIANS 2:12 NASB

*Whoever is not willing to carry the cross
and follow me is not worthy of me. Those who try
to hold on to their lives will give up true life.
Those who give up their lives for me
will hold on to true life.*

MATTHEW 10:38-39 NCV

A TIMELY TIP

Difficult people have a way of getting you off track. But when you follow in Christ's footsteps—when you honor Him with your thoughts, your actions, and your prayers—you can be sure that you're always on the right track.

40

FORGIVENESS

BE QUICK TO FORGIVE

Above all, love each other deeply,
because love covers a multitude of sins.
1 PETER 4:8 NIV

Even the most mild-mannered people will, on occasion, have reason to become frustrated by the inevitable shortcomings of family members, friends, and acquaintances. But wise men and women are quick to forgive others, just as God has forgiven them.

The commandment to forgive is clearly a part of God's Word, but oh how difficult a commandment it can be to follow. Because we are imperfect beings, we are quick to anger, quick to blame, slow to forgive, and even slower to forget. But even when forgiveness is difficult, God's instructions are straightforward: as Christians who have received the gift of forgiveness, we must now share that gift with others.

When we have been injured or embarrassed, we feel the urge to strike back and to hurt the people who have hurt us. Christ instructs us to do otherwise. We are taught that forgiveness is God's way and that mercy is an integral part of God's plan for our lives. In short, we are commanded to weave the thread of forgiveness into the very fabric of our lives.

Have you forgiven all the people who have done you harm (with no exceptions)? If so, you are to be congratulated. But if you hold bitterness against even a single person—even if that person is no longer living—it's now time to forgive.

Bitterness and regret are not part of God's plan for your life. Forgiveness is. And once you've forgiven others, you can then turn your thoughts to a far more pleasant subject: the incredibly bright future that God has in store for you.

MORE THOUGHTS ABOUT FORGIVENESS

Forgiveness is one of the most beautiful words in the human vocabulary. How much pain could be avoided if we all learned the meaning of this word!
BILLY GRAHAM

Forgiveness does not change the past, but it does enlarge the future.
DAVID JEREMIAH

Forgiveness is an act of the will, and the will can function regardless of the temperature of the heart.
CORRIE TEN BOOM

In one bold stroke, forgiveness obliterates the past and permits us to enter the land of new beginnings.
BILLY GRAHAM

More from God's Word

Judge not, and you shall not be judged.
Condemn not, and you shall not be condemned.
Forgive, and you will be forgiven.
Luke 6:37 NKJV

And whenever you stand praying,
if you have anything against anyone,
forgive him, so that your Father in heaven
may also forgive you your wrongdoing.
Mark 11:25 HCSB

But I say to you, love your enemies,
and pray for those who persecute you.
Matthew 5:44 NASB

And be kind to one another, tenderhearted,
forgiving one another, just as God in Christ forgave you.
Ephesians 4:32 NKJV

The merciful are blessed,
for they will be shown mercy.
Matthew 5:7 HCSB

A Timely Tip

When you're dealing with difficult people, remember this: forgiveness is its own reward, and bitterness is its own punishment. Guard your words and thoughts accordingly.

41

GOD'S ABUNDANCE

GOD WANTS YOU TO LIVE ABUNDANTLY

I have come that they may have life,
and that they may have it more abundantly.
JOHN 10:10 NKJV

God has a plan for every facet of your life, and His plan includes provision for your spiritual, physical, and emotional health. But He expects you to do your fair share of the work. In a world that is populated by imperfect people, you may find it all too easy to respond impulsively, thus making matters even worse. A far better strategy, of course, is to ask for God's guidance. And you can be sure that whenever you ask for God's help, He will give it.

God's Word promises that He will support you in good times and comfort you in hard times. The Creator of the universe stands ready to give you the strength to meet any challenge and the courage to deal effectively with difficult people. When you ask for God's help, He responds in His own way and at His own appointed hour. But make no mistake: He always responds.

Today, as you encounter the inevitable challenges of everyday life, remember that your heavenly Father never leaves you, not even for a moment. He's always available, always ready to listen, always ready to lead. When you make a habit of talking to Him early and often, He'll guide you and comfort you every day of your life.

MORE THOUGHTS ABOUT
GOD'S ABUNDANCE

God loves you and wants you to experience peace and life—abundant and eternal.
BILLY GRAHAM

God is the giver, and we are the receivers. And His richest gifts are bestowed not upon those who do the greatest things, but upon those who accept His abundance and His grace.
HANNAH WHITALL SMITH

Those who have been truly converted to Jesus Christ know the meaning of abundant living.
BILLY GRAHAM

Jesus wants Life for us; Life with a capital L.
JOHN ELDREDGE

The only way you can experience abundant life is to surrender your plans to Him.
CHARLES STANLEY

More from God's Word

Until now you have asked for nothing in My name.
Ask and you will receive, that your joy may be complete.
JOHN 16:24 HCSB

My cup runs over. Surely goodness and mercy
shall follow me all the days of my life;
and I will dwell in the house of the LORD forever.
PSALM 23:5–6 NKJV

And God is able to make all grace abound to you,
so that always having all sufficiency in everything,
you may have an abundance for every good deed.
2 CORINTHIANS 9:8 NASB

Success, success to you, and success to those
who help you, for your God will help you.
1 CHRONICLES 12:18 NIV

May Yahweh bless you and protect you; may Yahweh make
His face shine on you, and be gracious to you.
NUMBERS 6:24–25 HCSB

A Timely Tip

God's blessings are always available. Even when you're dealing with an unfortunate situation or a difficult person, the Lord is constantly offering you His abundance and His peace. So remember that you can still find peace amid the storm if you do your best and leave the rest up to Him.

42

GOD'S GUIDANCE

LET HIM DIRECT YOUR PATH

*Trust in the LORD with all your heart, and lean not
on your own understanding; in all your ways
acknowledge Him, and He shall direct your paths.*

PROVERBS 3:5–6 NKJV

If you're dealing with difficult people or troubling circumstances, you need God's guidance. And of this you can be sure: if you seek His guidance, He will give it.

C. S. Lewis observed, "I don't doubt that the Holy Spirit guides your decisions from within when you make them with the intention of pleasing God. The error would be to think that He speaks only within, whereas in reality He speaks also through Scripture, the Church, Christian friends, and books." These words remind us that God has many ways to make Himself known. Our challenge is to make ourselves open to His instruction.

Do you place a high value on God's guidance, and do you talk to Him regularly about matters great and small? Or do you talk with God on a haphazard basis? If you're wise, you'll form the habit of speaking to God early and often. But you won't stop there—you'll also study God's Word, you'll obey God's commandments, and you'll associate with people who do likewise.

So if you're unsure of your next step, lean upon God's promises and lift your prayers to Him. Remember that God is always near—always trying to get His message through. Open yourself to Him every day, and trust Him to guide your path. When you do, you'll be protected today, tomorrow, and forever.

More Thoughts about God's Guidance

As you walk through the valley of the unknown, you will find the footprints of Jesus both in front of you and beside you.
CHARLES STANLEY

When we are obedient, God guides our steps and our stops.
CORRIE TEN BOOM

God never leads us to do anything that is contrary to the Bible.
BILLY GRAHAM

Are you serious about wanting God's guidance to become a personal reality in your life? The first step is to tell God that you know you can't manage your own life; that you need His help.
CATHERINE MARSHALL

The will of God will never take us where the grace of God cannot sustain us.
BILLY GRAHAM

More from God's Word

Yet Lord, You are our Father; we are the clay,
and You are our potter; we all are the work of Your hands.
ISAIAH 64:8 HCSB

Show me thy ways, O Lord; teach me thy paths.
Lead me in thy truth, and teach me: for thou art the God
of my salvation; on thee do I wait all the day.
PSALM 25:4–5 KJV

The Lord says, "I will guide you along the best pathway
for your life. I will advise you and watch over you."
PSALM 32:8 NLT

Teach me to do Your will, for You are my God;
Your Spirit is good. Lead me in the land of uprightness.
PSALM 143:10 NKJV

Morning by morning he wakens me and opens my
understanding to his will. The Sovereign Lord
has spoken to me, and I have listened.
ISAIAH 50:4–5 NLT

A Timely Tip

When you're dealing with a difficult person, pray for guidance. When
you seek it, He will give it.

43

GOD'S HELP

TURN TO HIM FOR STRENGTH

So we can be sure when we say, "I will not be afraid, because the Lord is my helper. People can't do anything to me."
HEBREWS 13:6 NCV

Dealing with difficult people can be exhausting. That's one reason—but not the only reason—that you need God's help. God is not distant, and He is not disinterested. To the contrary, your heavenly Father is attentive to your needs. In fact, the Lord knows precisely what you need and when you need it. But He still wants to talk with you, and you most certainly need to talk to Him.

Jesus made it clear to His disciples: they should pray always. And so should we. Genuine, heartfelt prayer changes things and it changes us. When we lift our hearts to our Father in heaven, we open ourselves to a never-ending source of divine wisdom and infinite love.

Do you have questions that you simply can't answer? Ask for the guidance of your Creator. Whatever your need, no matter how great or small, pray about it. And remember: God is not just near; He is here, and He's ready to talk with you. Now!

More Thoughts about God's Help

Faith is not merely holding on to God.
It is God holding on to you.
CORRIE TEN BOOM

God will give us the strength
and resources we need to live through
any situation in life that He ordains.
BILLY GRAHAM

In God's faithfulness lies eternal security.
CORRIE TEN BOOM

Once we recognize our need for Jesus,
then the building of our faith begins.
It is a daily, moment-by-moment
life of absolute dependence upon Him for everything.
CATHERINE MARSHALL

More from God's Word

Peace, peace to you, and peace to him
who helps you, for your God helps you.
1 Chronicles 12:18 HCSB

Wait on the Lord, and He will rescue you.
Proverbs 20:22 HCSB

The Lord is my strength and my song;
He has become my salvation.
Exodus 15:2 HCSB

For I, Yahweh your God, hold your right hand
and say to you: Do not fear, I will help you.
Isaiah 41:13 HCSB

Ask, and it will be given to you; seek, and you will find;
knock, and it will be opened to you.
For everyone who asks receives, and he who seeks finds,
and to him who knocks it will be opened.
Matthew 7:7–8 NKJV

A Timely Tip

When you ask God for help, He will give it. So if there's something you really need—or a difficult person you need to deal with—pray about it. God is listening, and He wants to hear from you now.

44

GOD'S PLAN

TRUST HIS PLAN

*But as it is written: What eye did not see
and ear did not hear, and what never entered
the human mind—God prepared this for those who love Him.*
1 CORINTHIANS 2:9 HCSB

Why does God allow difficult people to cross our paths and disrupt our lives? He does it for specific reasons that are known only to Him, but of this we can be sure: the Lord has a plan, and He always has our best interests at heart.

God created our universe, and He rules it according to plans that are His and His alone. Through His Word, He makes promises that He will most certainly keep throughout eternity. But sometimes God's plans are simply impossible for us to understand. Why are some people burdened with difficult personalities? We can't be sure. And why do bad things happen to good people? We don't know. But God does. And we must trust His perfect plan even when we cannot understand it.

Your heavenly Father reigns over His creation, and He reigns over your little corner of that creation too. Your challenge is to recognize God's sovereignty and to trust His promises. Sometimes the Lord will not reveal Himself as quickly—or as clearly—as you would like. But rest assured: God is in control, and He desires to lead you along a path of His choosing. Your challenge is to trust, to listen, to learn, and to follow.

MORE THOUGHTS ABOUT GOD'S PLAN

*Every experience God gives us, every person
He brings into our lives, is the perfect preparation
for the future that only He can see.*
CORRIE TEN BOOM

*If not a sparrow falls upon the ground without
your Father, you have reason to see the smallest
events of your career are arranged by Him.*
C. H. SPURGEON

*God has no problems, only plans.
There is never panic in heaven.*
CORRIE TEN BOOM

*God's purpose is greater than our problems,
our pain, and even our sin.*
RICK WARREN

*God has a course mapped out for your life,
and all the inadequacies in the world will not change
His mind. He will be with you every step of the way.*
CHARLES STANLEY

More from God's Word

For My thoughts are not your thoughts, and your ways are not My ways....For as heaven is higher than earth, so My ways are higher than your ways, and My thoughts than your thoughts.
ISAIAH 55:8–9 HCSB

It is God who is at work in you, both to will and to work for His good pleasure.
PHILIPPIANS 2:13 NASB

And yet, O LORD, you are our Father. We are the clay, and you are the potter. We are all formed by your hand.
ISAIAH 64:8 NLT

For whoever does the will of God is My brother and My sister and mother.
MARK 3:35 NKJV

We must do the works of Him who sent Me while it is day. Night is coming when no one can work.
JOHN 9:4 HCSB

A Timely Tip

Even when times are tough, you can be sure that God has a wonderful plan for your life. And the time to start looking for that plan—and living it—is now. Discovering God's plan begins with prayer, but it doesn't end there. You've also got to work at it.

45

GOD'S POWER

GOD IS STRONGER
THAN DIFFICULT CIRCUMSTANCES
AND DIFFICULT PEOPLE

Depend on the LORD and his strength;
always go to him for help.
Remember the miracles he has done;
remember his wonders and his decisions.

PSALM 105:4–5 NCV

Of this you can be sure: God is sufficient to meet your needs. He is all-powerful; He is in control; and He loves you. Whatever hardships you may face, whatever heartbreaks you must endure, God is with you, and He stands ready to comfort you and to heal you.

If you are experiencing the intense pain of a difficult relationship or a recent loss, the Lord offers peace. Or if you are still mourning a loss from long ago, He can help you make peace with your past and move on. The loving heart of God is sufficient to meet any challenge, including yours. Trust the sufficiency of God.

More Thoughts about
God's Power

God is able to do what we can't do.
BILLY GRAHAM

To yield to God means to belong to God,
and to belong to God means to have
all His infinite power.
To belong to God means to have all.
HANNAH WHITALL SMITH

There is no limit to God.
There is no limit to His power.
There is no limit to His love.
There is no limit to His mercy.
BILLY GRAHAM

Of course you will encounter trouble.
But behold a God of power who can take
any evil and turn it into a door of hope.
CATHERINE MARSHALL

God's specialty is raising dead things to life
and making impossible things possible.
You don't have the need that exceeds His power.
BETH MOORE

More from God's Word

His divine power has given us everything we need
for a godly life through our knowledge of him
who called us by his own glory and goodness.
2 Peter 1:3 NIV

But Jesus looked at them and said, "With men this
is impossible, but with God all things are possible."
Matthew 19:26 HCSB

For the LORD your God is the God of gods
and Lord of lords, the great,
mighty, and awesome God.
Deuteronomy 10:17 HCSB

Is anything impossible for the LORD?
Genesis 18:14 HCSB

You are the God of great wonders!
You demonstrate your awesome power among the nations.
Psalm 77:14 NLT

A Timely Tip

When you're dealing with a difficult troublesome situation or a difficult person, think about God's strength and what it means to you. And while you're at it, think about the things that you and He, working together, can accomplish.

46

GOD'S PRESENCE

HE IS ALWAYS HERE

Draw near to God, and He will draw near to you.
JAMES 4:8 HCSB

Since God is everywhere, we are free to sense His presence whenever we take the time to quiet our souls and turn our prayers to Him. But sometimes, amid the incessant demands of life, we turn our thoughts far from God. When we do, we suffer.

Do you schedule a regular meeting each day with your Creator? You should. During those moments of stillness, you will gain direction, perspective, and peace—God's peace.

The comforting words of Psalm 46:10 remind us to "be still, and know that I am God" (NIV). When we do so, we sense the loving presence of our heavenly Father, and we are comforted by the certain knowledge that God is, quite literally, right here, right now. And He's ready to help. Right here, right now.

More Thoughts about God's Presence

It is God to whom and with whom we travel,
and while He is the end of our journey,
He is also at every stopping place.
ELISABETH ELLIOT

Mark it down. You will never go where God is not.
MAX LUCADO

God is an infinite circle
whose center is everywhere.
ST. AUGUSTINE

Do not limit the limitless God!
With Him, face the future unafraid
because you are never alone.
LETTIE COWMAN

The Lord is the one who travels
every mile of the wilderness way as our leader,
cheering us, supporting and
supplying and fortifying us.
ELISABETH ELLIOT

More from God's Word

*For the eyes of Yahweh roam throughout
the earth to show Himself strong
for those whose hearts are completely His.*
2 Chronicles 16:9 HCSB

*Though I walk through the valley
of the shadow of death,
I will fear no evil: for thou art with me.*
Psalm 23:4 KJV

Be still, and know that I am God.
Psalm 46:10 KJV

*I know the Lord is always with me.
I will not be shaken, for he is right beside me.*
Psalm 16:8 NLT

I am not alone, because the Father is with Me.
John 16:32 NKJV

A Timely Tip

God isn't far away—He's right here, right now. And He's willing to talk to you right here, right now.

47

GOD'S PROMISES

TRUST GOD'S PROMISES

As for God, his way is perfect: the word of the LORD is tried:
he is a buckler to all those that trust in him.

PSALM 18:30 KJV

In the eighteenth psalm, David teaches us that God is trustworthy. Simply put, when God makes a promise, He keeps it.

God's promises are found in a book like no other: the Holy Bible. The Bible is a roadmap for life here on earth and for life eternal. As Christians, we are called upon to trust its promises, to follow its commandments, and to share its Good News. If you're continually grappling with difficult people or unfortunate circumstance, you need a daily dose of faith, hope, and clear thinking. God's Word provides all three, and much, much more.

If we seek to follow in Christ's footsteps, we must study the Bible daily and meditate upon its meaning for our lives. Otherwise, we deprive ourselves of a priceless gift from our Creator. God's Holy Word is, indeed, a transforming, life-changing, one-of-a-kind treasure. And a passing acquaintance with the Good Book is insufficient for Christians who seek to obey God's Word and to understand His will.

More Thoughts about God's Promises

Let God's promises shine on your problems.
CORRIE TEN BOOM

The Bible is God's book of promises,
and unlike the books of man,
it does not change or go out of date.
BILLY GRAHAM

Gather the riches of God's promises.
Nobody can take away from you
those texts from the Bible
which you have learned by heart.
CORRIE TEN BOOM

Beloved, God's promises can never fail
to be accomplished, and those who
patiently wait can never be disappointed,
for a believing faith leads to realization.
LETTIE COWMAN

Don't let obstacles along the road to eternity
shake your confidence in God's promises.
DAVID JEREMIAH

More from God's Word

Let us hold on to the confession
of our hope without wavering,
for He who promised is faithful.
Hebrews 10:23 HCSB

My God is my rock, in whom I take refuge,
my shield and the horn of my salvation.
2 Samuel 22:3 NIV

Sustain me as You promised,
and I will live; do not let me be ashamed of my hope.
Psalm 119:116 HCSB

They will bind themselves to the Lord
with an eternal covenant
that will never again be broken.
Jeremiah 50:5 NLT

He heeded their prayer,
because they put their trust in him.
1 Chronicles 5:20 NKJV

A Timely Tip

God has made many promises to you, and He will keep every single one of them. Your job is to trust God's Word and to live accordingly.

48

GOD'S PROTECTION

HE IS OUR SHEPHERD IN GOOD TIMES AND DIFFICULT TIMES

The LORD is my shepherd, I shall not want.
He makes me lie down in green pastures;
He leads me beside quiet waters. He restores my soul.
PSALM 23:1–3 NASB

God knows everything about His creation. Whether we're enjoying happy days or challenging ones, the Creator watches over us and protects us.

The Lord is our greatest refuge. When every earthly support system fails, He remains steadfast, and His love remains unchanged. When we encounter life's inevitable disappointments and setbacks, the Father remains faithful. When we encounter trying circumstances or difficult people, He is always with us, always ready to respond to our prayers, always working in us and through us to turn trouble into triumph.

Thankfully, even when there's nowhere else to turn, we can turn our thoughts and prayers to the Lord, and He will respond. Even during life's most difficult days, God stands by us. Our job, of course, is to return the favor and stand by Him.

MORE THOUGHTS ABOUT GOD'S PROTECTION

Measure the size of the obstacles against the size of God.
BETH MOORE

Only believe, don't fear. Our Master,
Jesus, always watches over us,
and no matter what the persecution,
Jesus will surely overcome it.
LOTTIE MOON

A mighty fortress is our God,
a bulwark never failing,
our helper He amid the flood
of mortal ills prevailing.
MARTIN LUTHER

The safest place in all the world
is in the will of God, and the safest protection
in all the world is the name of God.
WARREN WIERSBE

As you walk through the valley of the unknown,
you will find the footprints of Jesus
both in front of you and beside you.
CHARLES STANLEY

More from God's Word

The Lord is my light and my salvation—
whom should I fear? The Lord is the stronghold
of my life—of whom should I be afraid?
PSALM 27:1 HCSB

Those who trust in the Lord are like Mount Zion.
It cannot be shaken; it remains forever.
PSALM 125:1 HCSB

As for God, His way is perfect; the word of the Lord is proven;
He is a shield to all who trust in Him.
PSALM 18:30 NKJV

The Lord is my rock, my fortress, and my deliverer, my God,
my mountain where I seek refuge. My shield, the horn of my
salvation, my stronghold, my refuge, and my Savior.
2 SAMUEL 22:2–3 HCSB

So we may boldly say: "The Lord is my helper;
I will not fear. What can man do to me?"
HEBREWS 13:6 NKJV

A Timely Tip

God has promised to protect you, and He's going to keep that promise. So if you're worried or afraid, pray for guidance and pray for a trusting heart. You need both, and He will give you both *if* you ask.

49

GOD'S PROVISION

GOD WILL PROVIDE,
SO DON'T BE DISCOURAGED

Be strong and courageous, and do the work.
Don't be afraid or discouraged,
for the LORD God, my God, is with you.
He will not fail you or forsake you.
1 CHRONICLES 28:20 NLT

In a world filled with more frustrations than we can count, God promises us that He is stronger than any challenge that we may face. The Lord offers peace amid the inevitable storms of life. Our job is to accept His peace.

God has promised to protect us, and He intends to fulfill that promise. When we encounter difficult people or troubling circumstances, God provides wisdom and hope. When we're tempted to strike back in anger, God's guidance is the ultimate armor. When we need answers, the Bible is our ultimate resource.

Will you allow God's Word to be your guidebook for every situation? I hope so, because when you do, you can live courageously, knowing that you possess the ultimate protection: God's infallible truth and His unfailing love for you.

More Thoughts about God's Provision

*We shouldn't think about ourselves
and how weak we are.
We should think about God and how strong He is.*
BILLY GRAHAM

*Our Lord never drew power from Himself;
He drew it always from His Father.*
OSWALD CHAMBERS

*God will give us the strength
and resources we need to live through
any situation in life that He ordains.*
BILLY GRAHAM

*God is sufficient for all our needs,
for every problem, for every difficulty,
for every broken heart, for every human sorrow.*
PETER MARSHALL

*God's all-sufficiency is a major.
Your inability is a minor.
Major in majors, not in minors.*
CORRIE TEN BOOM

More from God's Word

I will give you a new heart
and put a new spirit within you.
EZEKIEL 36:26 HCSB

Put on the full armor of God
so that you can stand against
the tactics of the Devil.
EPHESIANS 6:11 HCSB

Don't be afraid, because I am your God.
I will make you strong and will help you;
I will support you with my right hand that saves you.
ISAIAH 41:10 NCV

My grace is sufficient for you,
for My strength is made perfect in weakness.
2 CORINTHIANS 12:9 NKJV

God is my shield, saving those
whose hearts are true and right.
PSALM 7:10 NLT

A Timely Tip

Earthly security is an illusion. Your only real security comes from the loving heart of God. If you seek maximum protection, there's only one place you can receive it: from an infinite God.

50

GOD'S TIMING

TRUST HIS TIMING

Those who trust in the LORD are like Mount Zion.
It cannot be shaken; it remains forever.
PSALM 125:1 HCSB

If you're involved in a difficult relationship, you're undoubtedly anxious for things to improve. Quite naturally, you'd like for the other person to change in ways that would make the relationship satisfactory for both parties. Perhaps you've prayed about the relationship but seen no results. If so, keep praying, keep working, and be patient.

God answers our prayers. What God does not do is this: He does not always answer our prayers as soon as we might like, and He does not always answer our prayers by saying yes. God isn't an order taker, and He's not some sort of cosmic vending machine. Sometimes—even when we want something very badly—our loving heavenly Father responds to our requests by saying no, and we must accept His answer, even if we don't understand it.

God answers prayers not only according to our wishes but also according to His master plan. We cannot know that plan, but we can know the Planner. And we must trust His wisdom, His righteousness, and His love. Always.

MORE THOUGHTS ABOUT GOD'S TIMING

Waiting on God brings us to
the journey's end quicker than our feet.
LETTIE COWMAN

The Christian's journey through life
isn't a sprint but a marathon.
BILLY GRAHAM

We must learn to move according to the timetable
of the Timeless One, and to be at peace.
ELISABETH ELLIOT

Teach us, O Lord, the disciplines of patience,
for to wait is often harder than to work.
PETER MARSHALL

We often hear about waiting on God,
which actually means that He is waiting
until we are ready. There is another side,
however. When we wait for God,
we are waiting until He is ready.
LETTIE COWMAN

More from God's Word

*Therefore humble yourselves under the mighty hand of God,
that He may exalt you in due time.*
1 PETER 5:6 NKJV

*Trust in the LORD with all your heart, and lean not
on your own understanding; in all your ways acknowledge
Him, and He shall direct your paths.*
PROVERBS 3:5–6 NKJV

*He has made everything appropriate in its time.
He has also put eternity in their hearts, but man cannot
discover the work God has done from beginning to end.*
ECCLESIASTES 3:11 HCSB

*Yet the LORD longs to be gracious to you; therefore he will
rise up to show you compassion. For the LORD
is a God of justice. Blessed are all who wait for him!*
ISAIAH 30:18 NIV

*To every thing there is a season,
and a time to every purpose under the heaven.*
ECCLESIASTES 3:1 KJV

A Timely Tip

If you're waiting patiently for the Lord to help you resolve a difficult situation, remember this: God is never early or late; He's always on time. Although you don't know precisely what you need—or when you need it—He does. So trust His timing.

51

GOD'S WORD

LET HIS WORD BE YOUR LAMP

Your word is a lamp for my feet and a light on my path.
PSALM 119:105 HCSB

The Bible is a roadmap for life here on earth and for life eternal. As Christians, we are called upon to trust its promises, to follow its commandments, and to share its Good News.

As believers, we must study the Bible each day and meditate upon its meaning for our lives. Otherwise, we deprive ourselves of a priceless gift from our Creator. God's Holy Word is, indeed, a transforming, life-changing, one-of-a-kind treasure. And a passing acquaintance with the Good Book is insufficient for Christians who seek to obey God's Word and to understand His will.

God has made promises to mankind and to you. God's promises never fail and they never grow old. You must trust those promises and share them with your family, with your friends, and with the world.

As we face the inevitable challenges of life here on earth, we must arm ourselves with the promises of God's holy Word. When we do, we can expect the best, not only for the day ahead, but also for all eternity.

More Thoughts About God's Word

*Meditating upon His Word will inevitably bring
peace of mind, strength of purpose, and power for living.*
BILL BRIGHT

The Bible is the word of God from cover to cover.
BILLY SUNDAY

*The Bible is God's book of promises, and unlike
the books of man, it does not change or go out of date.*
BILLY GRAHAM

*The Bible grows more beautiful as we
grow in our understanding of it.*
JOHANN WOLFGANG VON GOETHE

*The Reference Point for the Christian is the Bible.
All values, judgments, and attitudes must be gauged
in relationship to this Reference Point.*
RUTH BELL GRAHAM

More from God's Word

*Jesus answered, "It is written: 'Man does not live on bread
alone, but on every word that comes from the mouth of God.'"*
MATTHEW 4:4 NIV

For the word of God is living and effective
and sharper than any double-edged sword, penetrating
as far as the separation of soul and spirit, joints and marrow.
It is able to judge the ideas and thoughts of the heart.

HEBREWS 4:12 HCSB

Therefore everyone who hears these words
of mine and puts them into practice is like
a wise man who built his house on the rock.

MATHEW 7:24–25 NIV

For in the gospel the righteousness of God is revealed—
a righteousness that is by faith from first to last,
just as it is written: "The righteous will live by faith."

ROMANS 1:17 NIV

All Scripture is given by inspiration of God,
and is profitable for doctrine, for reproof, for correction,
for instruction in righteousness, that the man of God may
be complete, thoroughly equipped for every good work.

2 TIMOTHY 3:16–17 NKJV

A TIMELY TIP

The Bible contains divine wisdom for dealing with difficult people and unfortunate circumstances. The Lord intends for you to use His Word as your guidebook for life. Your intentions should be the same.

52

GRIEF

HE OFFERS COMFORT

Weeping may endure for a night, but joy comes in the morning.
PSALM 30:5 NKJV

When you find yourself caught up in a troubling relationship with a difficult person, you may wonder if you'll ever escape the pain. When the feelings of anger or frustration are intense, you may think—mistakenly—that your problems will never end. But the good news is this: while time heals many wounds, God has the power to heal them all.

Ours is a God of infinite power and infinite possibilities. But sometimes, because of limited faith and limited understanding, we wrongly assume that God cannot or will not intervene in the affairs of everyday life. Such assumptions are simply wrong. The Lord is busily at work, constantly reshaping His world and your world. Your job is to ask Him—fervently and often—for the things you need.

Have you sincerely asked God for His help as you deal with the difficult people in your life? Have you asked Him to lead you and protect you? Have you prayed for the peace that passes all under-standing? If so, you're on the right track. If not, it's time to abandon your doubts and reclaim your faith in God's promises.

God's Word makes it clear: absolutely nothing is impossible for Him. So the next time you find yourself overwhelmed by difficult circumstances or difficult people, refocus your thoughts and redouble your prayers. Your challenge, as a believer, is to take God at His word, and to wait patiently for Him to bless you with the peace that flows from His miraculous healing touch.

MORE THOUGHTS ABOUT GRIEF

God is sufficient for all our needs,
for every problem, for every difficulty,
for every broken heart, for every human sorrow.
PETER MARSHALL

Despair is always the gateway of faith.
OSWALD CHAMBERS

If there is something we need more than
anything else during grief, it is a friend who stands with us,
who doesn't leave us. Jesus is that friend.
BILLY GRAHAM

God has enough grace to solve every dilemma you face,
wipe every tear you cry, and answer every question you ask.
MAX LUCADO

Your greatest ministry will most likely
come out of your greatest hurt.
RICK WARREN

More from God's Word

Blessed are the poor in spirit:
for theirs is the kingdom of heaven.
Blessed are they that mourn:
for they shall be comforted.
MATTHEW 5:3–4 KJV

Ye shall be sorrowful, but your sorrow
shall be turned into joy.
JOHN 16:20 KJV

The LORD is near to those who
have a broken heart.
PSALM 34:18 NKJV

He heals the brokenhearted
and binds up their wounds.
PSALM 147:3 HCSB

The LORD shall give thee rest
from thy sorrow, and from thy fear.
ISAIAH 14:3 KJV

A Timely Tip

Grief is not meant to be avoided or feared; it is meant to be worked through. Grief hurts, but denying your true feelings can hurt even more. With God's help, you can face your pain and move beyond it.

53

GUARD YOUR HEART

GUARD YOUR HEART

Guard your heart above all else, for it is the source of life.
PROVERBS 4:23 HCSB

Difficult people tempt us to respond in vindictive, aggressive ways. Yet God's Word is clear: we are to guard our hearts "above all else." So how should we respond to the prickly personalities that complicate our lives and rouse our emotions? We must react fairly, honestly, and maturely, and we must never betray our Christian beliefs.

Here in the twenty-first century, distractions, frustrations, and angry eruptions are woven into the fabric of everyday life. Many famous people seem to take pride in discourteous behavior, and social media has dramatically increased our contact with troubled personalities. As believers, we must remain vigilant. Not only must we resist Satan when he confronts us, but we must also avoid the people and the places where Satan can most easily tempt us.

Do you seek God's peace and His blessings? Then guard your heart above all else. When you encounter a difficult person and you're tempted to lash out in anger, hold your tongue. When you're faced with a difficult choice or a powerful temptation, seek God's counsel and trust the counsel He gives. When you're uncertain of your next step, take a deep breath, calm yourself, and follow in the footsteps of God's only begotten Son. Invite God into your heart and live according to His commandments. When you do, you will be blessed today and tomorrow and forever.

MORE THOUGHTS ABOUT GUARDING YOUR HEART

The insight that relates to God comes from purity of heart, not from clearness of intellect.
OSWALD CHAMBERS

Our battles are first won or lost in the secret places of our will in God's presence, never in full view of the world.
OSWALD CHAMBERS

Our fight is not against any physical enemy; it is against organizations and powers that are spiritual. We must struggle against sin all our lives, but we are assured we will win.
CORRIE TEN BOOM

There is no neutral ground in the universe: every square inch, every split second, is claimed by God and counterclaimed by Satan.
C. S. LEWIS

No matter how many pleasures Satan offers you, his ultimate intention is to ruin you. Your destruction is his highest priority.
ERWIN LUTZER

More from God's Word

The pure in heart are blessed, for they will see God.
MATTHEW 5:8 HCSB

Those who obey his commands live in him,
and he in them. And this is how we know that he lives in us:
We know it by the Spirit he gave us.
1 JOHN 3:24 NIV

Flee from youthful passions, and pursue righteousness,
faith, love, and peace, along with those
who call on the Lord from a pure heart.
2 TIMOTHY 2:22 HCSB

The peace of God, which surpasses all understanding,
will guard your hearts and minds through Christ Jesus.
PHILIPPIANS 4:7 NKJV

Finally, brothers and sisters, whatever is true,
whatever is noble, whatever is right, whatever is pure,
whatever is lovely, whatever is admirable if anything is
excellent or praiseworthy—think about such things.
PHILIPPIANS 4:8 NIV

A Timely Tip

God wants you to guard your heart from situations or from people who would drive you away from Him. He wants the best for you, and you should want the same for yourself.

54

GUILT

DON'T LET GUILT RULE YOUR LIFE

Blessed are those who don't feel guilty
for doing something they have decided is right.
ROMANS 14:22 NLT

Some people have a way of making you feel guilty, even when you have nothing to feel guilty about. These folks are master manipulators who seek to control your behavior by controlling your thoughts. Your task, simply put, is to keep them from hijacking your thoughts and your life.

Are you troubled by feelings of guilt, even after you've received God's forgiveness? Is someone still badgering you about mistakes you made long ago? Is someone causing you to focus so intently on yesterday that your vision of today is clouded? If so, you still have work to do—spiritual work. First, remember that if you've already asked God for His forgiveness, He has granted it. So instead of asking Him for forgiveness (again!) ask Him for acceptance and trust—acceptance of the past and trust in His plan for your life.

If you find yourself plagued by feelings of guilt or shame, consult God's survival guide: His holy Word. And as you do so, consider the following biblically based tips for overcoming those feelings of guilt once and for all:

1. Stop doing the things that make you feel guilty. How can you expect to not feel guilty if you should feel guilty? (Acts 26:20)
2. Ask God for forgiveness. When you ask for it, He will give it (1 John 1:9).
3. Ask forgiveness from the people you have harmed. This step is hard, but helpful. And even if the other folks cannot find it in their hearts to forgive you, you have the satisfaction of knowing you that you asked (Proverbs 28:13).
4. Forgive yourself. If you're no longer misbehaving, it's the right thing to do. And today is the right day to do it (Romans 14:22).
5. Get busy making the world a better place. Now that God has forgiven you, it's time for you to show your gratitude by serving Him (Matthew 23:11–12).

MORE THOUGHTS ABOUT GUILT

Forgiveness is an opportunity that God extended to us on the cross. When we accept His forgiveness and are willing to forgive ourselves, then we find relief.
BILLY GRAHAM

The redemption, accomplished for us by our Lord Jesus Christ on the cross at Calvary, is redemption from the power of sin as well as from its guilt. Christ is able to save all who come unto God by Him.
HANNAH WHITALL SMITH

The purpose of guilt is to bring us to Jesus. Once we are there, then its purpose is finished. If we continue to make ourselves guilty—to blame ourselves—then that is a sin in itself.

CORRIE TEN BOOM

More from God's Word

Be gracious to me, God, according to Your faithful love; according to Your abundant compassion, blot out my rebellion. Wash away my guilt, and cleanse me from my sin.

PSALM 51:1–2 HCSB

Create in me a pure heart, God, and make my spirit right again.

PSALM 51:10 NCV

Let us come near to God with a sincere heart and a sure faith, because we have been made free from a guilty conscience, and our bodies have been washed with pure water.

HEBREWS 10:22 NCV

Consider my affliction and rescue me, for I have not forgotten Your instruction.

PSALM 119:153 HCSB

A Timely Tip

People with troublesome personalities often use guilt as a means of imposing their will upon others. If you're being manipulated by guilt, remember this: if you've asked for God's forgiveness, He has already given it. And if He's forgiven you, that's all that really matters.

55

HAPPINESS

YES, YOU CAN BE HAPPY

Those who listen to instruction will prosper;
those who trust the LORD will be joyful.
PROVERBS 16:20 NLT

Even if you've encountered difficult circumstances—or if you find yourself mired in an unhealthy relationship—you still have so many things to celebrate. God wants you to experience His abundance, even when times are tough.

Happiness is learning how to deal with the inevitable disappointments of life without losing faith or hope. Of course, life is often challenging, but we must not be afraid. God loves us, and He will protect us. In times of hardship, He will comfort us; in times of sorrow, He will dry our tears. When we are troubled or weak or sorrowful, God is always with us. We must build our lives on the rock that cannot be shaken: we must trust in God. And then we must get on with the hard work of tackling our problems...because if we don't, who will?

Do you seek happiness, abundance, and contentment? If so, here are some things you should do: Love God and His Son; depend upon God for strength; try, to the best of your abilities, to follow God's will; and strive to obey His holy Word. When you do these things, you'll discover that happiness goes hand in hand with righteousness. The happiest people are not those who rebel against God; the happiest people are those who love God and obey His commandments, even when it's hard.

More Thoughts about Happiness

Happiness is a thing that comes and goes.
It can never be an end in itself. Holiness,
not happiness, is the end of man.
Oswald Chambers

The truth is that even in the midst of trouble,
happy moments swim by us every day,
like shining fish waiting to be caught.
Barbara Johnson

The practical effect of Christianity is happiness,
therefore let it be spread abroad everywhere!
C. H. Spurgeon

Happy is the person who has learned the secret
of being content with whatever life brings him.
Billy Graham

Joy comes not from what we have but what we are.
C. H. Spurgeon

More from God's Word

If they obey and serve him,
they will spend the rest of their days
in prosperity and their years in contentment.
JOB 36:11 NIV

A joyful heart is good medicine,
but a broken spirit dries up the bones.
PROVERBS 17:22 HCSB

I have come that they may have life,
and that they may have it more abundantly.
JOHN 10:10 NKJV

Happiness makes a person smile,
but sadness can break a person's spirit.
PROVERBS 15:13 NCV

Joyful is the person who finds wisdom,
the one who gains understanding.
PROVERBS 3:13 NLT

A Timely Tip

The best day to be happy is this one. Even if you're dealing with a difficult situation, you have many reasons to celebrate, so don't delay; let the celebration begin today.

56

HATE

HATE EQUALS DARKNESS

He who says he is in the light,
and hates his brother, is in darkness until now.
1 JOHN 2:9 NKJV

In Deuteronomy 5:17, God issued a familiar commandment: "Thou shall not kill"(KJV). But Jesus went much further—He instructed us that anger and hatred are akin to murder:

> You have heard that our ancestors were told, "You must not murder. If you commit murder, you are subject to judgment." But I say, if you are even angry with someone, you are subject to judgment!
> Matthew 5:21–22 NLT

If you're like most people, you know a thing or two about anger—and maybe even a thing or two about hatred. Sometimes it's easy to become angry, and it's just as easy to hold a grudge. But God does not want your heart to be hardened by bitterness. He has far better plans for you.

So if you bear bitterness against anyone, take your bitterness to

God and leave it there. If you are angry, pray for God's healing hand to calm your spirit. If you are troubled by some past injustice, read God's Word and remember His commandment to forgive.

When you follow that commandment and sincerely forgive those who have hurt you, you'll discover that a heavy burden has been lifted from your shoulders. And you'll discover that although forgiveness is indeed difficult, with God's help, all things are possible.

More Thoughts about Hate

*Jesus had a loving heart. If He dwells within us,
hatred and bitterness will never rule us.*
Billy Graham

*Life is certainly too brief to waste
even a single moment on animosity.*
Cardinal Joseph Bernadine

*Give me such love for God and men
as will blot out all hatred and bitterness.*
Dietrich Bonhoeffer

*To hold on to hate and resentments is to throw
a monkey wrench into the machinery of life.*
E. Stanley Jones

*Love makes everything lovely; hate concentrates
itself on the one thing hated.*
George MacDonald

More from God's Word

You have heard that it was said, "Love your neighbor
and hate your enemy." But I tell you,
love your enemies and pray for those who persecute you,
that you may be children of your Father in heaven.
MATTHEW 5:43–45 NIV

Everyone must be quick to hear, slow to speak, and slow to
anger, for man's anger does not accomplish God's righteousness.
JAMES 1:19-20 HCSB

My dear brothers and sisters, always be willing to listen
and slow to speak. Do not become angry easily, because anger
will not help you live the right kind of life God wants.
JAMES 1:19–20 NCV

If anyone claims, "I am living in the light," but hates
a fellow believer, that person is still living in darkness.
1 JOHN 2:9 NLT

Do not be conquered by evil, but conquer evil with good.
ROMANS 12:21 HCSB

A Timely Tip

Life's too short to spend it hating anybody. And hatred is a spiritual sickness. So don't spend another moment holding a grudge against any person, alive or dead. God wants you to forgive everybody, no exceptions.

57

HOPE

NEVER LOSE HOPE

Let us hold fast the confession of our hope without wavering,
for He who promised is faithful.
HEBREWS 10:23 NASB

If you're dealing with a difficult person or enduring difficult circumstances, you may be discouraged and you may be exhausted. But if you're a Christian, there's never a valid reason to give up hope.

God's promises give us hope: hope for today, hope for tomorrow, hope for all eternity. The hope that the world offers is temporary, at best. But the hope that God offers never grows old and never goes out of date. It's no wonder, then, that when we pin our hopes on worldly resources, we are often disappointed. Be thankful that God has no such record of failure.

The Bible teaches that the Lord blesses those who trust in His wisdom and follow in the footsteps of His Son. Will you count yourself among that number? When you do, you'll have every reason on earth—and in heaven—to be hopeful about your future. After all, God has made important promises to you, promises that He is certainly going to keep. So be hopeful, be optimistic, be faithful, and do your best. Then, leave the rest up to God. Your destiny is safe with Him.

More Thoughts about Hope

Of course you will encounter trouble.
But behold a God of power who can take
any evil and turn it into a door of hope.
CATHERINE MARSHALL

Jesus gives us hope because
He keeps us company, has a vision,
and knows the way we should go.
MAX LUCADO

The presence of hope in the invincible
sovereignty of God drives out fear.
JOHN PIPER

The earth's troubles fade
in the light of heaven's hope.
BILLY GRAHAM

If your hopes are being disappointed just now,
it means that they are being purified.
OSWALD CHAMBERS

More from God's Word

This hope we have as an anchor of the soul,
a hope both sure and steadfast.
HEBREWS 6:19 NASB

Hope deferred makes the heart sick.
PROVERBS 13:12 NKJV

I say to myself, "The LORD is mine, so I hope in him."
LAMENTATIONS 3:24 NCV

The LORD is good to those who wait for Him,
to the soul who seeks Him. It is good that one should
hope and wait quietly for the salvation of the LORD.
LAMENTATIONS 3:25–26 NKJV

Be strong and courageous,
all you who put your hope in the LORD.
PSALM 31:24 HCSB

A Timely Tip

If you're worried about dealing with a difficult person or resolving a troublesome situation, be hopeful. You and God, working together, can do amazing things.

58

IMPULSIVITY

DON'T RUSH TO BE ANGRY

Don't let your spirit rush to be angry,
for anger abides in the heart of fools.
ECCLESIASTES 7:9 HCSB

When you encounter a person who possesses a difficult personality, do you respond without thinking? Do you react first and think about your reaction second? Are you simply a little too hotheaded for your own good? If so, God's Word has some advice for you.

The Bible teaches us to be self-controlled, thoughtful, and mature. But the world often tempts us to behave otherwise. Everywhere we turn, or so it seems, we see undisciplined, unruly role models who behave impulsively yet experience few, if any, negative consequences. So it's not surprising that when we meet folks whose personalities conflict with our own, we're tempted to respond in undisciplined, unruly ways. But there's a catch: if we fall prey to immaturity or impulsivity, those behaviors inevitably cause us many more problems than they solve.

Our impulses often lead us astray, but our heavenly Father never will. So if you're wise, you'll learn to slow yourself down, take a deep breath, and consult God before you strike out in anger, not after.

More Thoughts about Impulsivity

Patience is the companion of wisdom.
ST. AUGUSTINE

Zeal without knowledge is fire without light.
THOMAS FULLER

We must learn to wait.
There is grace supplied to the one who waits.
LETTIE COWMAN

Nothing is more terrible than activity without insight.
THOMAS CARLYLE

In times of uncertainty, wait.
Always, if you have any doubt, wait.
Do not force yourself to any action.
If you have a restraint in your spirit,
wait until all is clear, and do not go against it.
LETTIE COWMAN

More from God's Word

Enthusiasm without knowledge is no good;
haste makes mistakes.
PROVERBS 19:2 NLT

A patient spirit is better than a proud spirit.
ECCLESIASTES 7:8 HCSB

Do you see a man who speaks too soon?
There is more hope for a fool than for him.
PROVERBS 29:20 HCSB

Those who guard their lips preserve their lives,
but those who speak rashly will come to ruin.
PROVERBS 13:3 NIV

A prudent person foresees danger
and takes precautions; the simpleton goes
blindly on and suffers the consequences.
PROVERBS 22:3 NLT

A Timely Tip

In dealing with difficult people, sometimes the smartest thing you can do is to slow down and think before you act. When you take time to think and pray, you'll probably make smarter choices and give better responses.

59

INTEGRITY

BE GUIDED BY HONESTY

Good people will be guided by honesty;
dishonesty will destroy those who are not trustworthy.
PROVERBS 11:3 NCV

Lasting relationships are built upon a firm foundation of honesty and trust. Temporary relationships are built upon the shifting sands of deception and insincerity. If you're wise, you'll insist on relationships that are built on a firm foundation of mutual trust.

It has been said on many occasions that honesty is the best policy. But for Christians, it is far more important to note that honesty is God's policy.

Sometimes honesty is difficult; sometimes honesty is painful; sometimes honesty makes us feel uncomfortable. Despite these temporary feelings of discomfort, we must make honesty the hallmark of all our relationships; otherwise, we invite needless suffering and stress into our own lives and into the lives of those we love.

Sometime soon, perhaps even today, you may encounter someone who encourages you to bend the truth or to break it. Resist that temptation. Truth is God's way, and it must be your way too.

More Thoughts about Integrity

*Integrity is the glue that
holds our way of life together.*
BILLY GRAHAM

*The commandment of absolute
truthfulness is only another name
for the fullness of discipleship.*
DIETRICH BONHOEFFER

*The single most important element
in any human relationship is honesty—
with oneself, with God, and with others.*
CATHERINE MARSHALL

*True greatness is not measured
by the headlines or wealth.
The inner character of a person
is the true measure of lasting greatness.*
BILLY GRAHAM

*Let your words be the
genuine picture of your heart.*
JOHN WESLEY

More from God's Word

The one who lives with integrity lives securely,
but whoever perverts his ways will be found out.
PROVERBS 10:9 HCSB

Dishonest scales are detestable to the LORD,
but an accurate weight is His delight.
PROVERBS 11:1 HCSB

The good people who live honest lives
will be a blessing to their children.
PROVERBS 20:7 NCV

A righteous man is careful in dealing with his neighbor,
but the ways of wicked men lead them astray.
PROVERBS 12:26 HCSB

Let your "Yes" be "Yes," and your "No," 'No."
MATTHEW 5:37 NKJV

A Timely Tip

Honesty is the best policy because it's God's policy. It's up to you, and you alone, to make sure that you're always truthful, even when telling the truth is difficult.

60

JOY

DON'T LET ANYONE STEAL YOUR JOY

Rejoice always, pray without ceasing,
in everything give thanks;
for this is the will of God in Christ Jesus for you.
1 THESSALONIANS 5:16–18 NKJV

Have you made the choice to rejoice even when times are tough and people are being difficult? I hope so. After all, as a believer, you have many reasons to be joyful. Yet sometimes, amid the inevitable hustle and bustle of life here on earth, you may lose sight of your blessings as you wrestle with the challenges of everyday life.

Psalm 100 reminds us that, as believers, we have every reason to celebrate: "Shout for joy to the LORD, all the earth. Worship the LORD with gladness" (vv. 1–2 NIV).

If you find yourself feeling discouraged, angry, frustrated, or worse, it's time to slow down and have a quiet conversation with your Creator. If your heart is heavy, open the door of your soul to the Father and to His only begotten Son. Christ offers you His peace and His joy. Accept it and share it freely, just as Christ has freely shared His joy with you.

More Thoughts about Joy

Joy is the direct result of having
God's perspective on our daily lives
and the effect of loving our Lord
enough to obey His commands
and trust His promises.

Bill Bright

Joy comes not from what
we have but what we are.

C. H. Spurgeon

Joy is the great note all throughout the Bible.

Oswald Chambers

Joy is the settled assurance that
God is in control of all the details
of my life, the quiet confidence
that ultimately everything is going
to be all right, and the determined
choice to praise God in all things.

Kay Warren

Joy is the serious business of heaven.

C. S. Lewis

More from God's Word

This is the day which the LORD has made;
let us rejoice and be glad in it.
PSALM 118:24 NASB

Until now you have asked for nothing
in My name. Ask and you will receive,
that your joy may be complete.
JOHN 16:24 HCSB

Rejoice in the Lord always. Again I will say, rejoice!
PHILIPPIANS 4:4 NKJV

I have spoken these things to you so that My joy
may be in you and your joy may be complete.
JOHN 15:11 HCSB

So you also have sorrow now. But I will see you again.
Your hearts will rejoice, and no one will rob you of your joy.
JOHN 16:22 HCSB

A Timely Tip

Joy does not depend upon your circumstances; it depends upon your thoughts and upon your relationship with the Lord. Guard your heart and your thoughts accordingly.

61

JUDGING OTHERS

LET GOD BE THE JUDGE

Judge not, and you shall not be judged. Condemn not, and you shall not be condemned. Forgive, and you will be forgiven.
LUKE 6:37 NKJV

It's not surprising that we're quick to judge people with difficult personalities. The need to critique others seems woven into the very fabric of human consciousness. We mortals feel compelled to serve as informal judges and juries, pronouncing our own verdicts on the actions and perceived motivations of others, all the while excusing—and oftentimes hiding—our own shortcomings. But God's Word instructs us to let Him be the judge. He knows that we, with our limited knowledge and personal biases, are simply ill-equipped to assess the actions of others. The act of judging, then, becomes not only an act of futility, but also an affront to our Creator.

When Jesus came upon a woman who had been condemned by the Pharisees, He spoke not only to the people who had gathered there, but also to all generations. Christ warned, "He that is without sin among you, let him first cast a stone at her" (John 8:7 KJV). The message is clear: because we are all sinners, we must refrain from the temptation to judge others.

So the next time you're tempted to cast judgment on another human being, resist that temptation. God hasn't called you to be a judge; He's called you to be a witness.

MORE THOUGHTS ABOUT JUDGING OTHERS

Oh, how horrible our sins look when
they are committed by someone else.
CHARLES SWINDOLL

Don't judge other people more harshly
than you want God to judge you.
MARIE T. FREEMAN

We must learn to regard people
less in the light of what they do or omit to do,
and more in light of what they suffer.
DIETRICH BONHOEFFER

Yes, let God be the Judge.
Your job today is to be a witness.
WARREN WIERSBE

Judging draws the judgment of others.
CATHERINE MARSHALL

More from God's Word

Don't criticize one another, brothers.
He who criticizes a brother or judges his brother criticizes
the law and judges the law. But if you judge the law,
you are not a doer of the law but a judge.
JAMES 4:11 HCSB

Those who guard their lips preserve their lives,
but those who speak rashly will come to ruin.
PROVERBS 13:3 NIV

Therefore, any one of you who judges is without excuse.
For when you judge another, you condemn yourself,
since you, the judge, do the same things.
ROMANS 2:1 HCSB

Let the words of my mouth and the meditation
of my heart be acceptable in Your sight,
O LORD, my strength and my Redeemer.
PSALM 19:14 NKJV

A Timely Tip

It's easy to judge people who possess problematic personalities. But if you spend all day judging other people, you've wasted your day. So if you catch yourself being overly judgmental, slow down long enough to interrupt those critical thoughts before they hijack your emotions and wreck your day.

62

KEEP LEARNING

DIFFICULT PEOPLE HAVE LESSONS TO TEACH US

Wisdom is the principal thing; therefore get wisdom.
And in all your getting, get understanding.
PROVERBS 4:7 NKJV

God sometimes uses difficult people to achieve His plans for our lives. The folks with prickly personalities have much to teach us about ourselves, so we should examine every encounter to determine if God is using our adversaries to advance our own spiritual growth. If we're open to God's instruction, we have much to learn. For example, difficult people can teach us about spiritual virtues such as forgiveness, courage, and patience. Oftentimes our antagonists provide us with valuable lessons we could learn no other way.

When it comes to learning life's most important lessons, we can either do things the easy way or the hard way. The easy way can be summed up as follows: when God teaches us a lesson, we learn it...the first time. Unfortunately, too many of us learn much more slowly than that.

When we resist God's instruction, He continues to teach, whether we like it or not. Our challenge, then, is to discern God's lessons from the experiences of everyday life. Hopefully, we learn those lessons sooner rather than later because the sooner we do, the sooner He can move on to the next lesson, and the next, and the next.

More Thoughts about Learning from Difficult People

True learning can take place at every age of life,
and it doesn't have to be in the curriculum plan.
Suzanne Dale Ezell

Life is not a holiday but an education.
And, the one eternal lesson
for all of us is how we can love.
Henry Drummond

Every day we live is a priceless
gift of God, loaded with possibilities
to learn something new, to gain fresh insights.
Dale Evans Rogers

Learning makes a man fit company for himself.
Thomas Fuller

A time of trouble and darkness is meant
to teach you lessons you desperately need.
Lettie Cowman

More from God's Word

Commit yourself to instruction;
listen carefully to words of knowledge.
PROVERBS 23:12 NLT

Teach me Your way, Yahweh,
and I will live by Your truth.
Give me an undivided mind to fear Your name.
PSALM 86:11 HCSB

Enthusiasm without knowledge is not good.
If you act too quickly, you might make a mistake.
PROVERBS 19:2 NCV

Joyful is the person who finds wisdom,
the one who gains understanding.
PROVERBS 3:13 NLT

Anyone who listens to my teaching
and obeys me is wise, like a person
who builds a house on solid rock.
MATTHEW 7:24 NLT

A Timely Tip

When we're dealing with difficult people, we can sometimes learn lessons about ourselves that we could learn in no other way. So when you encounter a person with a prickly personality, ask yourself this question: What lesson do I need to learn from this experience?

63

KINDNESS
AND COMPASSION

DO THE RIGHT THING
AND DON'T LOSE HEART

*And let us not grow weary while doing good,
for in due season we shall reap if we do not lose heart.*
GALATIANS 6:9 NKJV

As Christians, we have certain rules that we must live by. One of those rules is the Golden Rule, which instructs us to treat others as we wish to be treated. It's a simple concept to understand but a decidedly more difficult concept to put into practice, especially when people are behaving badly. Nonetheless, we are instructed to be kind and compassionate to all people, not just the ones who are easy to get along with.

Today, as you consider all the things that Christ has done in your life, honor Him by being a little kinder than necessary. Honor Him by slowing down long enough to say an extra word of encouragement to someone who needs it. Honor Him by picking up the phone and calling a distant friend…for no reason other than to say, "I'm thinking of you." Honor Christ by following His commandment and obeying the Golden Rule. He expects no less, and He deserves no less.

More Thoughts about Kindness and Compassion

Want to snatch a day from the manacles of boredom?
Do overgenerous deeds, acts beyond reimbursement.
Kindness without compensation.
Do a deed for which you cannot be repaid.
MAX LUCADO

One of the greatest things a man can do for his
heavenly Father is to be kind to some of His other children.
HENRY DRUMMOND

When we bring sunshine into the lives of others,
we're warmed by it ourselves.
When we spill a little happiness, it splashes on us.
BARBARA JOHNSON

All around you are people whose lives are filled with trouble
and sorrow. They need your compassion and encouragement.
BILLY GRAHAM

Do all the good you can by all the means you can
in all the places you can at all the times you can
to all the people you can as long as ever you can.
JOHN WESLEY

More from God's Word

*Therefore, whatever you want men to do to you,
do also to them, for this is the Law and the Prophets.*
MATTHEW 7:12 NKJV

*Be kind to one another, tender-hearted,
forgiving each other, just as God in Christ also has forgiven you.*
EPHESIANS 4:32 NASB

*A new commandment I give unto you,
That ye love one another; as I have loved you,
that ye also love one another.*
JOHN 13:34 KJV

*Who is wise and has understanding among you?
He should show his works
by good conduct with wisdom's gentleness.*
JAMES 3:13 HCSB

*Assuredly, I say to you, inasmuch as you did it
to one of the least of these My brethren, you did it to Me.*
MATTHEW 25:40 NKJV

A Timely Tip

The Golden Rule starts with you, so be kind to everybody, even the people with prickly personalities. Be sure to treat them in the same way that you would like to be treated if you were in their shoes.

64

LIFE

EVEN WHEN TIMES ARE TOUGH, STAY ON COURSE

I urge you to live a life worthy of the calling you have received.
EPHESIANS 4:1 NIV

Life can be tough sometimes, but it's also wonderful; it's a glorious gift from God. How will you use that gift? Will you treat this day as a precious treasure from your heavenly Father, or will you take the next twenty-four hours for granted? The answer should be obvious: every day, including this one, comes gift wrapped from God. Your job is to unwrap that gift, to use it wisely, and to give thanks to the Giver.

Each waking moment holds the potential to celebrate, to serve, to share, or to love. Because you are a person with incalculable potential, each moment has incalculable value. Your challenge is to experience each day to the full as you seek to live in accordance with God's plan for your life. When you do, you'll experience His abundance and His peace.

Even when you're working your way through difficult circumstances or troubling relationships, you have much to celebrate. So with no further delay, let the celebration begin. After all, today is already here, and it will soon be gone. The rest is up to you.

More Thoughts about Life

Live out your life in its full meaning; it is God's life.
JOSIAH ROYCE

Wherever you are, be all there.
Live to the hilt every situation
you believe to be the will of God.
JIM ELLIOT

The measure of a life, after all,
is not its duration but its donation.
CORRIE TEN BOOM

You have life before you. Only you can live it.
HENRY DRUMMOND

You can't control the length of your life—
but you can control its width and depth.
JOHN MAXWELL

More from God's Word

You will teach me how to live a holy life.
Being with you will fill me with joy;
at your right hand I will find pleasure forever.
PSALM 16:11 NCV

Jesus said to her, "I am the resurrection
and the life. The one who believes
in Me, even if he dies, will live.
Everyone who lives and believes in Me
will never die—ever. Do you believe this?"
JOHN 11:25–26 HCSB

Whoever finds their life will lose it,
and whoever loses their life for my sake will find it.
MATTHEW 10:39 NIV

And Jesus said unto them,
I am the bread of life:
he that cometh to me shall never hunger;
and he that believeth on me shall never thirst.
JOHN 6:35 KJV

He who follows righteousness
and mercy finds life, righteousness and honor.
PROVERBS 21:21 NKJV

A TIMELY TIP

Your life is a priceless opportunity, a gift of incalculable worth. Be thankful to the Giver and use His gift wisely. And don't let anyone rob you of the joy that can—and should—be yours.

65

LISTENING TO GOD

LISTEN AND LEARN

Come to me with your ears wide open.
Listen, and you will find life.
ISAIAH 55:3 NLT

If you have questions, God has answers. And if you have problems, God has solutions. If you're looking for His guidance, all you need do is ask.

Sometimes God speaks loudly and clearly. More often He speaks in a quiet voice—and if you are wise, you will be listening carefully when He does. To do so, you must carve out quiet moments each day to study His Word and sense His direction.

Can you quiet yourself long enough to listen to your conscience? Are you attuned to the subtle guidance of your intuition? Are you willing to pray sincerely and then to wait quietly for God's response? I hope so. Usually God refrains from sending His messages on stone tablets or city billboards. More often He communicates in subtler ways. If you sincerely desire to hear His voice, you must listen carefully, and you must do so in the silent corners of your quiet, willing heart.

More Thoughts about Listening to God

If you, too, will learn to wait upon God,
to get alone with Him, and remain silent
so that you can hear His voice when
He is ready to speak to you,
what a difference it will make in your life!

Kay Arthur

Deep within the center of the soul
is a chamber of peace where
God lives and where, if we will
enter it and quiet all the other sounds,
we can hear His gentle whisper.

Lettie Cowman

When God speaks to us,
He should have our full attention.
Billy Graham

Prayer begins by talking to God,
but it ends in listening to him. In the face of
Absolute Truth, silence is the soul's language.

Fulton J. Sheen

God's voice is still and quiet
and easily buried under an avalanche of clamor.

Charles Stanley

MORE FROM GOD'S WORD

Be still, and know that I am God.
PSALM 46:10 KJV

*The one who is from God
listens to God's words.
This is why you don't listen,
because you are not from God.*
JOHN 8:47 HCSB

*In quietness and in confidence
shall be your strength.*
ISAIAH 30:15 KJV

*Rest in the LORD,
and wait patiently for Him.*
PSALM 37:7 NKJV

Be silent before Me.
ISAIAH 41:1 HCSB

A TIMELY TIP

In every stage of life, and in every circumstance, God has important things He's trying to teach you. So listen carefully to your conscience; pay attention to the things you learn in the Bible; and try to learn something new every day. When you do, God will guide you and protect you.

66

LOVE

WE'RE INSTRUCTED TO LOVE
ALL PEOPLE (EVEN THE DIFFICULT ONES)

*You have heard that it was said, "Love your neighbor
and hate your enemy." But I tell you, love your enemies
and pray for those who persecute you, that you
may be children of your Father in heaven.*

MATTHEW 5:43–45 NIV

So what should we do about the difficult people who inhabit our lives
and invade our psyches? First, we should remember that as Christians
we're instructed to love everybody, even our enemies. Sometimes that
might seem like an impossible task, but it's not.

Are you easily frustrated by the inevitable imperfections of others?
Are you easily angered? Do you sometimes hold on to feelings of
bitterness and regret? If so, perhaps you need a refresher course in
the art of forgiveness.

Bitterness will consume your life if you let it. Hatred will rob
you of peace. The search for revenge will leave you frustrated. The
only peace that lasts is God's peace, which is available only to those
who make the choice to forgive. Sometimes forgiveness is a hard
choice to make, but the rewards are always worth the sacrifice. If

we are to follow in Christ's footsteps, we must love one another, no exceptions.

MORE THOUGHTS ABOUT LOVE

Love is not getting, but giving.
HENRY VAN DYKE

Love always means sacrifice.
ELISABETH ELLIOT

The vast ocean of Love
cannot be measured or explained,
but it can be experienced.
SARAH YOUNG

Line by line, moment by moment,
special times are etched into our
memories in the permanent ink
of everlasting love in our relationships.
GLORIA GAITHER

Love does not dominate; it cultivates.
JOHANN WOLFGANG VON GOETHE

More from God's Word

A new commandment I give unto you,
That ye love one another; as I have loved you,
that ye also love one another.

JOHN 13:34 KJV

Above all, love each other deeply,
because love covers a multitude of sins.

1 PETER 4:8 NIV

Love is patient, love is kind. Love does not envy,
is not boastful, is not conceited.

1 CORINTHIANS 13:4 HCSB

Beloved, if God so loved us,
we ought also to love one another.

1 JOHN 4:11 KJV

And we have known and believed the love
that God has for us. God is love, and he who abides
in love abides in God, and God in him.

1 JOHN 4:16 NKJV

A Timely Tip

Today, think about someone you know who, for whatever reason, is difficult to love. Then you think of a good way to express your love for that person, even if you'd rather express some other less favorable emotion.

67

MIRACLES

EXPECT A MIRACLE

Is anything too hard for the LORD?
GENESIS 18:14 NKJV

Sometimes, because we are imperfect human beings with limited understanding and limited faith, we place limitations on God. But God's power has no limitations. God will work miracles in our relationships and our lives if we trust Him with everything we have and everything we are. When we do, we experience the miraculous results of His endless love and His awesome power.

Miracles, both great and small, are an integral part of everyday life, but usually we are too busy or too cynical to notice God's handiwork. We don't expect to see miracles, so we simply overlook them.

Do you lack the faith that God can work miracles in your own life? Do you doubt, even for a moment, that God can repair your relationships and cleanse your heart? If so, it's time to reconsider. If you have allowed yourself to become a "doubting Thomas," you are attempting to place limitations on a God who has none. Instead of doubting your heavenly Father, you must trust Him. Then you must wait and watch because something miraculous is going to happen to you, and it might just happen today.

More Thoughts about God's Power to Work Miracles

God specializes in things thought impossible.
CATHERINE MARSHALL

*It is wonderful what miracles
God works in wills that are
utterly surrendered to Him.*
HANNAH WHITALL SMITH

*God's faithfulness and grace
make the impossible possible.*
SHEILA WALSH

*Faith means believing in realities
that go beyond sense and sight.
It is the awareness of unseen
divine realities all around you.*
JONI EARECKSON TADA

God is able to do what we can't do.
BILLY GRAHAM

More from God's Word

*And God confirmed the message by
giving signs and wonders and various miracles
and gifts of the Holy Spirit whenever he chose.*
HEBREWS 2:4 NLT

*You are the the God of great wonders!
You demonstrate your awesome power among the nations.*
PSALM 77:14 NLT

*No eye has seen, no ear has heard,
no mind has imagined what God
has prepared for those who love him.*
1 CORINTHIANS 2:9 NIV

*And Jesus looking upon them saith,
With men it is impossible,
but not with God:
for with God all things are possible.*
MARK 10:27 KJV

For with God nothing shall be impossible.
LUKE 1:37 KJV

A Timely Tip
Never be afraid to hope—or to ask—for a miracle.

68

MISTAKES

MISTAKES HAPPEN: WE SHOULD LEARN FROM THEM AND MOVE ON

He who covers his sins will not prosper, but whoever confesses and forsakes them will have mercy.
PROVERBS 28:13 NKJV

Everybody makes mistakes, and so will you. It's inevitable: When you're dealing with difficult people, you won't be able to manage those relationships perfectly. Despite your best efforts, you'll probably be dragged into problematic circumstances that will be frustrating or heartbreaking or both. And then you may be tempted to blame yourself for the problem. If you find yourself in that situation, please remember that nobody's perfect, including you.

Winston Churchill once observed, "Success is going from failure to failure without loss of enthusiasm." What was good for Churchill is also good for you. You should expect to make mistakes—plenty of mistakes—but you should not allow those inevitable missteps to rob you of the enthusiasm you need to fulfill God's plan for your life.

We are imperfect people living in an imperfect world; mistakes are simply part of the price we pay for being here. But even though mistakes are an inevitable part of life's journey, repeated mistakes should not be. When we find ourselves in a problematic relationship, we must take steps to correct the problems, to learn from them, and to pray for the wisdom not to repeat them. When we do, our mistakes become lessons, and our lives become adventures in growth, not stagnation.

Have you made a mistake or two while dealing with a difficult person? Of course you have. But here's the big question: Have you used your mistakes as stumbling blocks or stepping stones? The answer to that question will determine the quality of your future relationships and the quality of your life.

MORE THOUGHTS ABOUT MISTAKES

*By the mercy of God, we may repent a wrong choice
and alter the consequences by making a right choice.*
A. W. TOZER

*Mistakes offer the possibility for redemption
and a new start in God's kingdom. No matter what
you're guilty of, God can restore your innocence.*
BARBARA JOHNSON

*God is able to take mistakes, when they are committed to Him,
and make of them something for our good and for His glory.*
RUTH BELL GRAHAM

It is human to err, but it is devilish to remain willfully in error.
ST. AUGUSTINE

More from God's Word

*If we confess our sins to him, he is faithful and just
to forgive us and to cleanse us from all wickedness.*
1 John 1:9 NLT

Be merciful, just as your Father is merciful.
Luke 6:36 NIV

*Therefore let us approach the throne of grace
with boldness, so that we may receive mercy
and find grace to help us at the proper time.*
Hebrews 4:16 HCSB

*But the mercy of the Lord is from everlasting
to everlasting upon them that fear him,
and his righteousness unto children's children.*
Psalm 103:17 KJV

*Therefore, if anyone is in Christ, he is a new creation;
old things have passed away; behold, all things have become new.*
2 Corinthians 5:17 NKJV

A Timely Tip

When you're dealing with a difficult person, don't expect the results to be perfect. And don't expect your relationship with them to be perfect either. Their difficult personality may make it impossible to have a smooth, trouble-free relationship. So when you come to a speedbump in one of your relationships, don't be surprised or discouraged. And if you make a mistake, forgive yourself. Immediately.

69

NEGATIVE PEER PRESSURE

SAYING NO TO
NEGATIVE PEER PRESSURE

*Do not be mismatched with unbelievers. For what partnership
is there between righteousness and lawlessness?
Or what fellowship does light have with darkness?*
2 CORINTHIANS 6:14 HCSB

Peer pressure can be a good thing or a bad thing, depending upon
your peers. If your peers encourage you to live truthfully—and if
they encourage you to follow God's will and to obey His commandments—then you'll experience positive peer pressure, and that's
good. But if you are involved with people who encourage you to do
foolish things—or immoral things—you're facing a different kind
of peer pressure: the negative kind.

Rick Warren observed, "Those who follow the crowd usually
get lost in it." We know those words to be true, but oftentimes
we fail to live by them. Instead of trusting God for guidance, we
imitate our friends and suffer the consequences. Instead of seeking
to please our Father in heaven, we strive to please our peers, with
decidedly mixed results. Instead of doing the right thing, we do the
"easy" thing or the "popular" thing. And when we do, we pay a high
price for our shortsightedness.

Would you like a time-tested formula for successful living? Here is a simple formula that is proven and true: Don't give in to negative peer pressure. Period. Instead of getting lost in the crowd, you should find guidance from God. Does this sound too simple? Perhaps it is simple, but it is also the only way to reap all the marvelous riches that God has in store for you.

MORE THOUGHTS ABOUT PEER PRESSURE

Fashion is an enduring testimony to the fact that we live quite consciously before the eyes of others.
JOHN ELDREDGE

Character is always lost when a high ideal is sacrificed on the altar of conformity and popularity.
CHARLES SWINDOLL

Many Christians give in to various temptations through peer pressure. They find themselves surrendering to worldly passions, justifying pleasures the world offers.
BILLY GRAHAM

Those who follow the crowd usually get lost in it. I don't know all the keys to success, but one key to failure is to try to please everyone.
RICK WARREN

More from God's Word

Do not be deceived: "Bad company corrupts good morals."
1 Corinthians 15:33 HCSB

Do you think I am trying to make people accept me?
No, God is the One I am trying to please.
Am I trying to please people? If I still wanted
to please people, I would not be a servant of Christ.
Galatians 1:10 NCV

Dear friend, do not imitate what is evil,
but what is good. The one who does good is of God;
the one who does evil has not seen God.
3 John 1:11 HCSB

But Peter and the apostles replied,
"We must obey God rather than men."
Acts 5:29 HCSB

My son, if sinners entice you, don't be persuaded.
Proverbs 1:10 HCSB

A Timely Tip

Peer pressure can be good or bad. God wants you to seek out the good and flee from the bad. So if you encounter someone who encourages you to behave badly—or who encourages you to betray your conscience—run, don't walk, in the opposite direction.

70

NEGATIVITY

SAY NO TO NEGATIVITY

In my distress I prayed to the LORD,
and the LORD answered me and set me free.
PSALM 118:5 NLT

Some people are beset by chronic, severe, immutable negativity. These folks focus so intently on the inevitable problems of life that they fail to see the blessings and opportunities that surround them. And as a result of their negativity, they create emotional roadblocks for themselves *and* for the people they influence.

Negativity is highly contagious: we give it to others who, in turn, give it back to us. Thankfully, this cycle can be broken by positive thoughts, heartfelt prayers, and encouraging words.

As English clergyman William Ralph Inge observed, "No Christian should be a pessimist, for Christianity is a system of radical optimism." Inge's observation is true, of course, but sometimes you may find yourself caught up in the emotional quicksand of a negative person whose unhealthy attitude has infected yours. When you find yourself manufacturing negative thoughts that are not based on God's truth, it's time to slow down, collect yourself, refocus your thoughts, count your blessings, and talk to God.

The Lord has made many promises to you, and He will most certainly keep every one of them. So you have every reason to be an optimist and no legitimate reason to ever abandon hope. So today and every day, trust your hopes, not your fears. And while you're at it, take time to celebrate God's blessings. His gifts are too numerous to calculate and too glorious to imagine. But it never hurts to try.

MORE THOUGHTS ABOUT OVERCOMING NEGATIVITY

Avoid arguments, but when a negative attitude is expressed, counter it with a positive and optimistic opinion.
NORMAN VINCENT PEALE

Developing a positive attitude means working continually to find what is uplifting and encouraging.
BARBARA JOHNSON

The things we think are the things that feed our souls. If we think on pure and lovely things, we shall grow pure and lovely like them; and the converse is equally true.
HANNAH WHITALL SMITH

We choose what attitudes we have right now. And it's a continuing choice.
JOHN MAXWELL

More from God's Word

I say to myself, "The Lord is mine, so I hope in him."
LAMENTATIONS 3:24 NCV

*The Lord is good to those who wait for Him,
to the soul who seeks Him. It is good
that one should hope and wait quietly
for the salvation of the Lord.*
LAMENTATIONS 3:25–26 NKJV

Hope deferred makes the heart sick.
PROVERBS 13:12 NKJV

*Be strong and courageous,
all you who put your hope in the Lord.*
PSALM 31:24 HCSB

Make me to hear joy and gladness.
PSALM 51:8 KJV

A Timely Tip

Positive thinking breeds more positive thinking, and negative thinking breeds more negative thinking. So nip negativity in the bud, starting today and continuing every day of your life.

71

NEW BEGINNINGS

THE PAINS AND THE
JOYS OF STARTING OVER

Then the One seated on the throne said,
"Look! I am making everything new."
REVELATION 21:5 HCSB

If you've recently extricated yourself from a difficult relationship—or if you've been forced to cut ties with someone whose personality was simply too problematic to endure—you may feel like you're entering a new phase of life. Your fresh start is an occasion to remember that God has a perfect plan for your life, and that He has the power to make all things new.

As you think about your future—and as you consider the countless opportunities that will be woven into the fabric of the days ahead—be sure to include God in your plans. When you do, He will guide your steps and light your path.

Lasting change doesn't occur "out there"; it occurs "in here." It occurs, not in the shifting sands of your own particular circumstances, but in the quiet depths of your own obedient heart. So if you're in search of a new beginning or, for that matter, a new you, don't expect changing circumstances to miraculously transform you into the person you want to become. Transformation starts with God, and it starts in the silent center of a humble human heart—like yours.

MORE THOUGHTS ABOUT NEW BEGINNINGS

What saves a man is to take a step. Then another step.
C. S. LEWIS

*Each day you must say to yourself,
"Today I am going to begin."*
JEAN PIERRE DE CAUSSADE

*The best preparation for the future is the present
well seen to, and the last duty done.*
GEORGE MACDONALD

*Are you in earnest? Seize this very minute.
What you can do, or dream you can, begin it.
Boldness has genius, power, and magic in it.*
JOHANN WOLFGANG VON GOETHE

MORE FROM GOD'S WORD

*Do not remember the former things, nor consider
the things of old. Behold, I will do a new thing.*
ISAIAH 43:18–19 NKJV

There is one thing I always do.
Forgetting the past and straining toward
what is ahead, I keep trying to reach the goal
and get the prize for which God called me.
PHILIPPIANS 3:13–14 NCV

Your old sinful self has died,
and your new life is kept with Christ in God.
COLOSSIANS 3:3 NCV

You are being renewed in the spirit of your minds;
you put on the new self, the one created according to God's
likeness in righteousness and purity of the truth.
EPHESIANS 4:23–24 HCSB

"For I know the plans I have for you"—
this is the LORD's declaration—"plans for your welfare,
not for disaster, to give you a future and a hope."
JEREMIAH 29:11 HCSB

A TIMELY TIP

Sometimes, despite our best efforts, relationships must end and we must move on. If you're enduring the pain of a recent breakup—or living with painful memories of an old relationship gone bad—remember that God has the power to make all things new, including you. So if you're graduating into a new phase of life, be sure to make God your partner. If you do, He'll guide your steps; He'll help carry your burdens; and, He'll help you focus on the opportunities of the future, not the losses of the past.

72

PAINFUL EXPERIENCES

WHEN YOU'RE SUFFERING

And the God of all grace, who called you to his eternal glory in Christ, after you have suffered a little while, will himself restore you and make you strong, firm and steadfast.
1 PETER 5:10 NIV

All of us face times of adversity. When we face the inevitable difficulties of life here on earth, we can seek help from family, from friends, and from God. God's love remains constant. The Lord remains ready to comfort us and strengthen us whenever we turn to Him. The Bible promises, "The LORD is near to all who call upon Him, to all who call upon Him in truth. He will fulfill the desire of those who fear Him; He also will hear their cry and save them. The LORD preserves all who love Him" (Psalm 145:18–20 NKJV). This comforting passage reminds us that when we are troubled, we should call upon God, and in time, He will heal us. And until He does, we may be comforted in the knowledge that we never suffer alone.

Barbara Johnson writes, "There is no way around suffering. We have to go through it to get to the other side." The best way to "get to the other side" of suffering is to get there with God. When we turn open hearts to Him in heartfelt prayer, He will answer in His own time and according to His own plan. And while we are waiting for God's plan to unfold and for His healing touch to restore us, we can be comforted in the knowledge that our Creator can overcome any obstacle, even if we cannot.

MORE THOUGHTS ABOUT PAINFUL EXPERIENCES

The promises of God's Word sustain us in our suffering,
and we know Jesus sympathizes and empathizes
with us in our darkest hour.
BILL BRIGHT

Suffering is never for nothing. It is that you and
I might be conformed to the image of Christ.
ELISABETH ELLIOT

You don't have to be alone in your hurt! Comfort is yours.
Joy is an option. And it's all been made possible by your Savior.
JONI EARECKSON TADA

God is sufficient for all our needs, for every problem, for every
difficulty, for every broken heart, for every human sorrow.
PETER MARSHALL

God whispers to us in our pleasures,
speaks in our conscience, but shouts in our pains:
it is His megaphone to rouse a deaf world.
C. S. LEWIS

More from God's Word

Is anyone among you suffering? He should pray.
JAMES 5:13 HCSB

In my distress I called upon the LORD,
and cried unto my God: he heard my voice.
PSALM 18:6 KJV

I have told you these things so that in Me you may have peace.
You will have suffering in this world.
Be courageous! I have conquered the world.
JOHN 16:33 HCSB

You who are now hungry are blessed, because you will be filled.
You who now weep are blessed, because you will laugh.
LUKE 6:21 HCSB

I have heard your prayer;
I have seen your tears. Look, I will heal you.
2 KINGS 20:5 HCSB

A Timely Tip

All of us must, from time to time, deal with difficult people. And sometimes we must endure unfortunate circumstances that test our faith. No man or woman, no matter how righteous, is exempt. Christians, however, face their grief with the ultimate armor: God's promises. God will help heal us if we invite Him into our hearts.

73

PAST

MAKE PEACE WITH YOUR PAST

*One thing I do, forgetting those things which
are behind and reaching forward to those things
which are ahead, I press toward the goal for the prize
of the upward call of God in Christ Jesus.*

PHILIPPIANS 3:13–14 NKJV

Because you are human, you may be slow to forget yesterday's disappointments. But if you sincerely seek to focus your hopes and energies on the future, then you must find ways to accept the past, no matter how difficult it may be to do so.

Have you made peace with your past? If so, congratulations. But if you are mired in the quicksand of bitterness or regret, it's time to plan your escape. How can you do so? By accepting what has been and by trusting God for what will be. You must also forgive those who have hurt you and learn the lessons that hard times have taught you.

So if you have not yet made peace with the past, today is the day to declare an end to all hostilities. When you do, you can then turn your thoughts to the wondrous promises of God and to the glorious future that He has in store for you.

More Thoughts about Making Peace with Your Past

Our yesterdays present irreparable things to us;
it is true that we have lost opportunities which
will never return, but God can transform this destructive
anxiety into a constructive thoughtfulness for the future.

Oswald Chambers

Trust the past to God's mercy, the present to God's love,
and the future to God's providence.

St. Augustine

Don't waste energy regretting the way things are
or thinking about what might have been.
Start at the present moment—accepting things
exactly as they are—and search for
My way in the midst of those circumstances.

Sarah Young

Don't be bound by the past and its failures.
But don't forget its lessons either.

Billy Graham

Who you are in Christ is far more
important and meaningful than whatever
has taken place in your past.

Elizabeth George

MORE FROM GOD'S WORD

*Do not remember the former things, nor consider
the things of old. Behold, I will do a new thing.*
ISAIAH 43:18–19 NKJV

*He restoreth my soul: he leadeth me in the paths
of righteousness for his name's sake.*
PSALM 23:3 KJV

*Have mercy on me, O God, according to your unfailing love;
according to your great compassion blot out my transgressions.
Wash away all my iniquity and cleanse me from my sin.*
PSALM 51:1–2 NIV

*Your old sinful self has died, and your new life
is kept with Christ in God.*
COLOSSIANS 3:3 NCV

*And He who sits on the throne said,
"Behold, I am making all things new."*
REVELATION 21:5 NASB

A TIMELY TIP

The past is past. Don't invest all your mental energy there. If you're focusing on yesterday, it's time to change your focus. If you're living in the past, move on while there's still time. If you're bearing a grudge against someone, it's time to forgive.

74

PATIENCE

PATIENCE IS POWERFUL

A person's wisdom gives him patience;
it is to one's glory to overlook an offense.
PROVERBS 19:11 NIV

Time and again, God's Word teaches us to be patient and kind. We are commanded to love our neighbors, even when our neighbors aren't very neighborly. But being mere mortals, we sometimes fall short. We become easily frustrated with the shortcomings of others even though we are remarkably tolerant of our own failings.

We live in an imperfect world inhabited by imperfect friends, imperfect acquaintances, and imperfect strangers. Sometimes we inherit troubles from these imperfect people, and sometimes we create troubles by ourselves. In either case, what's required is patience: patience for other people's shortcomings as well as our own.

Proverbs 16:32 teaches, "Better to be patient than powerful; better to have self-control than to conquer a city" (NLT). But for most of us, patience is difficult. We'd rather strike back than hold back. However, God has other plans. He instructs us to be patient, kind, and helpful to the people He places along our path. He instructs us to love our neighbors, even the ones who are chronically hard to live with. As believers, we must strive to obey Him, even when it's hard.

More Thoughts about the Power of Patience

Bear with the faults of others
as you would have them bear with yours.
PHILLIPS BROOKS

Patience graciously, compassionately,
and with understanding judges
the faults of others without unjust criticism.
BILLY GRAHAM

Patience is the companion of wisdom.
ST. AUGUSTINE

Today, take a complicated situation and with time,
patience, and a smile, turn it into
something positive—for you and for others.
JONI EARECKSON TADA

Frustration is not the will of God.
There is time to do anything and everything
that God wants us to do.
ELISABETH ELLIOT

More from God's Word

Patience of spirit is better than haughtiness of spirit.
ECCLESIASTES 7:8 NASB

Be joyful in hope,
patient in affliction,
faithful in prayer.
ROMANS 12:12 NIV

Better to be patient than powerful;
better to have self-control than to conquer a city.
PROVERBS 16:32 NLT

But if we hope for what we do not yet have,
we wait for it patiently.
ROMANS 8:25 NIV

The Lord is good to those who depend on him,
to those who search for him.
So it is good to wait quietly
for salvation from the Lord.
LAMENTATIONS 3:25–26 NLT

A Timely Tip

In dealing with difficult situations or problematic people, patience pays. Impatience costs. Behave accordingly.

75

PEACE

GOD WANTS YOU
TO EXPERIENCE PEACE

*These things I have spoken to you, that in Me
you may have peace. In the world you will have tribulation;
but be of good cheer, I have overcome the world.*
JOHN 16:33 NKJV

When you encounter someone who possesses a problematic personality, it's up to you, and nobody else, to maintain your peace of mind. Of course, the other person's unpleasant attitude may make your job harder. After all, difficult people have a way of ruffling our emotions and distorting our thoughts. But with God's help, and with a little common sense, we can find peace amid the emotional storm.

Life is too short to allow another person's bad attitude to invade your psyche and ruin your day. But because human emotions are contagious, there's always the danger that you'll be drawn into the other person's mental state, with predictably negative consequences.

A far better strategy is to step back from the situation, to say a silent prayer, and to ask God to help you retain a sense of calm. When you do, He'll answer your prayer, the storm will pass, and you'll be glad you retained your emotional stability, even though the people around you were losing theirs.

MORE THOUGHTS ABOUT EXPERIENCING GOD'S PEACE

When something robs you of your peace of mind,
ask yourself if it is worth the energy you are expending on it.
If not, then put it out of your mind in an act of discipline.
Every time the thought of "it" returns, refuse it.
KAY ARTHUR

Peace does not mean to be in a place where
there is no noise, trouble, or hard work.
Peace means to be in the midst of all
those things and still be calm in your heart.
CATHERINE MARSHALL

In the center of a hurricane there is
absolute quiet and peace. There is no safer
place than in the center of the will of God.
CORRIE TEN BOOM

God's power is great enough for our
deepest desperation. You can go on.
You can pick up the pieces and start anew.
You can face your fears. You can find peace in the rubble.
There is healing for your soul.
SUZANNE DALE EZELL

MORE FROM GOD'S WORD

Peace I leave with you, My peace I give to you;
not as the world gives do I give to you. Let not your heart
be troubled, neither let it be afraid.
JOHN 14:27 NKJV

But the fruit of the Spirit is love, joy, peace,
patience, kindness, goodness, faith, gentleness, self-control.
Against such things there is no law.
GALATIANS 5:22–23 HCSB

He Himself is our peace.
EPHESIANS 2:14 NASB

The peace of God, which passeth all understanding,
shall keep your hearts and minds through Christ Jesus.
PHILIPPIANS 4:7 KJV

"I will give peace, real peace, to those far and near,
and I will heal them," says the LORD.
ISAIAH 57:19 NCV

A TIMELY TIP

Sometimes peace can be a scarce commodity, especially if you're dealing with someone who has a problematic personality. But God's peace is always available when you turn everything over to Him. No problem is too problematic for Him.

76

PERSEVERANCE

DON'T GIVE UP AND DON'T GIVE IN

Let us not become weary in doing good,
for at the proper time we will
reap a harvest if we do not give up.
GALATIANS 6:9 NIV

As you continue to seek God's purpose for your life, you will undoubtedly experience your fair share of disappointments, detours, and difficult people. When you do, don't become discouraged: God's not finished with you yet.

The old saying is as true today as it was when it was first spoken: "Life is a marathon, not a sprint." That's why wise travelers (like you) select a traveling companion who never tires and never falters. That partner, of course, is your heavenly Father.

The next time you find your courage tested by someone with a prickly personality, remember that God is as near as your next breath, and remember that He offers strength and comfort to His children. He is your shield and your strength; He is your protector and your deliverer. Call upon Him in your hour of need and then be comforted. Whatever your challenge, whatever your trouble, God can help you persevere. And that's precisely what He'll do if you ask

Him. Whatever your problem, God can handle it. Your job is to keep persevering until He does.

MORE THOUGHTS ABOUT PERSEVERANCE

Perseverance is not a passive submission
to circumstances—it is a strong
and active response to the difficult events of life.
ELIZABETH GEORGE

Everyone gets discouraged. The question is:
Are you going to give up or get up? It's a choice.
JOHN MAXWELL

Perseverance is more than endurance.
It is endurance combined with absolute
assurance and certainty that what
we are looking for is going to happen.
OSWALD CHAMBERS

Patience and diligence, like faith, remove mountains.
WILLIAM PENN

Success or failure can be pretty well predicted
by the degree to which the heart is fully in it.
JOHN ELDREDGE

More from God's Word

But as for you, be strong; don't be discouraged,
for your work has a reward.
2 Chronicles 15:7 HCSB

For you have need of endurance,
so that when you have done the will of God,
you may receive what was promised.
Hebrews 10:36 NASB

We are hard-pressed on every side,
yet not crushed; we are perplexed, but not in despair.
2 Corinthians 4:8 NKJV

Finishing is better than starting.
Patience is better than pride.
Ecclesiastes 7:8 NLT

So let us run the race that is before us and never give up.
We should remove from our lives anything that would
get in the way and the sin that so easily holds us back.
Hebrews 12:1 NCV

A Timely Tip

When you are tested, don't quit at the first sign of trouble. Instead, call upon God. He can give you the strength to persevere, and that's exactly what you should ask Him to do.

77

PERSPECTIVE

KEEP THINGS IN PERSPECTIVE

*Since you have been raised to new life with Christ,
set your sights on the realities of heaven, where Christ
sits in the place of honor at God's right hand.*

COLOSSIANS 3:1 NLT

For most of us, life is busy and complicated. Amid the rush and crush of the daily grind, it is easy to lose perspective...easy, but wrong. When our lives seem to have been hijacked by difficult people and the world seems to be spinning out of control, we can regain perspective by slowing ourselves down and then turning our thoughts and prayers toward God.

Do you carve out quiet moments each day to offer thanksgiving and praise to your Creator? You should. During these moments of stillness, you will often sense the love and wisdom of our Lord. When you call upon the Lord and prayerfully seek His will, He will give you wisdom and perspective. When you make God's priorities your priorities, He will direct your steps and calm your fears. So today and every day hereafter, pray for a sense of balance and perspective. And remember: no challenges are too big for God—and that includes yours.

More Thoughts about Maintaining Perspective

God's peace and perspective are
available to you through His Word.
ELIZABETH GEORGE

Joy is the direct result of having God's
perspective on our daily lives and the effect
of loving our Lord enough to obey
His commands and trust His promises.
BILL BRIGHT

Perspective is everything when
you are experiencing the challenges of life.
JONI EARECKSON TADA

To change ourselves effectively,
we first had to change our perceptions.
STEPHEN R. COVEY

The world appears very little to a soul
that contemplates the greatness of God.
BROTHER LAWRENCE

More from God's Word

Joyful is the person who finds wisdom,
the one who gains understanding.
PROVERBS 3:13 NLT

Teach me, LORD, the meaning of Your statutes,
and I will always keep them.
PSALM 119:33 HCSB

If you teach the wise,
they will get knowledge.
PROVERBS 21:11 NCV

The one who acquires good sense
loves himself; one who safeguards
understanding finds success.
PROVERBS 19:8 HCSB

Trust in the LORD with all your heart
and lean not on your own understanding.
PROVERBS 3:5 NIV

A Timely Tip

Being obedient to God means that you can't always please other people. Sometimes you've got to please God, no matter what anybody else says. People come and go, but God's love lasts forever. So don't worry about pleasing people. Worry about pleasing God.

78

PLEASING EVERYBODY IS IMPOSSIBLE

YOU CAN'T PLEASE EVERYBODY (NOR SHOULD YOU TRY)

For am I now trying to win the favor of people, or God?
Or am I striving to please people? If I were still trying
to please people, I would not be a slave of Christ.
GALATIANS 1:10 HCSB

If you're like most people, you'd like to gain the admiration and friendship of your neighbors, your coworkers, and, most importantly, your family members. Some people, however, are impossible to please, and other people want you to please them by doing things that are contrary to your faith.

It's perfectly okay to please other people, but your eagerness to please others should never overshadow your eagerness to please God.

Would you like a time-tested formula for successful relationships? Here is a formula that is proven and true: In every relationship you establish, seek God's approval first. Does this sound too simple? Perhaps it is simple, but it is also the only way to reap the marvelous riches that the Lord has in store for you.

The nineteenth-century reformer Margaret Fuller warned, "Beware of over-great pleasure in being popular or even beloved." And her words still ring true.

Few things in life are more futile than trying to please other people for the wrong reasons. When we place God in a position of secondary importance, we do ourselves great harm. But when we imitate Jesus and place the Lord in His rightful place—at the center of our lives—then we claim spiritual treasures that will endure forever.

Who will you try to please today: God or man? Your primary obligation is not to please imperfect men and women. Your obligation is to strive diligently to meet the expectations of an all-knowing and perfect God. Trust Him always. Love Him always. Praise Him always. And seek to please Him. Always.

MORE THOUGHTS ABOUT PLEASING PEOPLE

Popularity is far more dangerous for the Christian than persecution.
BILLY GRAHAM

The major problem with letting others define you is that it borders on idolatry. Your concern to please others dampens your desire to please your Creator.
SARAH YOUNG

If pleasing people is your goal, you will be enslaved to them. People can be harsh taskmasters when you give them this power over you.
SARAH YOUNG

More from God's Word

The fear of man is a snare,
but the one who trusts in the LORD is protected.
PROVERBS 29:25 HCSB

Keep your eyes focused on what is right,
and look straight ahead to what is good.
PROVERBS 4:25 NCV

It is better to take refuge in the LORD
than to trust in man.
PSALM 118:8 HCSB

My son, if sinners entice you, don't be persuaded.
PROVERBS 1:10 HCSB

Do not be unequally yoked together with unbelievers.
For what fellowship has righteousness
with lawlessness? And what communion
has light with darkness?
2 CORINTHIANS 6:14 NKJV

A Timely Tip

If you are burdened with a people-pleasing personality, outgrow it. Realize that you can't please all of the people all of the time, nor should you attempt to.

79

POSSIBILITIES

DEALING WITH DIFFICULT PEOPLE: IT'S HARD, BUT POSSIBLE

*I can do all things through Christ
which strengtheneth me.*
PHILIPPIANS 4:13 KJV

All of us face difficult days, and we all encounter difficult people from time to time. Sometimes even the most optimistic Christians can become discouraged, and you are no exception. If you find yourself enduring difficult circumstances, perhaps it's time for an extreme intellectual makeover—perhaps it's time to focus more on your strengths and opportunities, and less on the challenges that confront you.

Every day, including this one, is brimming with possibilities. Every day is filled with opportunities to grow, to serve, to share, and to rise above unfortunate situations. But if you are entangled in a web of negativity, you may overlook the blessings that God has scattered along your path. So don't give in to pessimism, to doubt, or to cynicism. Instead, keep your eyes upon the possibilities, fix your heart upon the Creator, do your best, and let Him handle the rest.

More Thoughts about Possibilities

I have found that there are three stages
in every great work of God:
first, it is impossible,
then it is difficult, then it is done.
Hudson Taylor

A possibility is a hint from God.
Søren Kierkegaard

God's specialty is raising dead things
to life and making impossible things possible.
You don't have the need that exceeds His power.
Beth Moore

Alleged "impossibilities" are opportunities
for our capacities to be stretched.
Charles Swindoll

We are all faced with a series of great opportunities
brilliantly disguised as impossible situations.
Charles Swindoll

More from God's Word

But Jesus looked at them and said to them,
"With men this is impossible,
but with God all things are possible."
MATTHEW 19:26 NKJV

Therefore we do not lose heart. Even though
our outward man is perishing, yet the
inward man is being renewed day by day.
2 CORINTHIANS 4:16 NKJV

Jesus said to him, "If you can believe,
all things are possible to him who believes."
MARK 9:23 NKJV

The things which are impossible with men
are possible with God.
LUKE 18:27 KJV

Is anything too hard for the LORD?
GENESIS 18:14 KJV

A Timely Tip

Dealing with tough situations and difficult people can be frustrating, time-consuming, and stressful, but with God's help, you're up to the challenge. Keep praying and keep trying to do the right thing. And remember: with Him, all things are possible.

80

PRAYING FOR
A PEACEFUL HEART

PRAY FOR PEACE OF MIND

Be anxious for nothing, but in everything
by prayer and supplication, with thanksgiving,
let your requests be made known to God.
PHILIPPIANS 4:6 NKJV

When you're dealing with a difficult person, it's easy to become frustrated. But even in the most difficult circumstances, God offers His peace if you ask for it. The beautiful words of John 14:27 remind us that Jesus offers us peace, not as the world gives, but as He alone gives: "Peace I leave with you. My peace I give to you. I do not give to you as the world gives. Your heart must not be troubled or fearful" (HCSB). Our challenge is to accept Christ's peace and then, as best we can, to share His peace with our neighbors.

Today, as a gift to yourself, to your family, and to your friends, claim the inner peace that is your spiritual birthright: the peace of Jesus Christ. It is offered freely; it has been paid for in full; it is yours for the asking. So ask. And then share.

As you go about your daily activities, remember God's instructions: "Rejoice always! Pray constantly. Give thanks in everything, for this is God's will for you in Christ Jesus" (1 Thessalonians 5:16–18 HCSB). Start praying in the morning and keep praying until you drop off to sleep at night. And rest assured: God is always listening, and He always wants to hear from you.

MORE THOUGHTS ABOUT PRAYING FOR A PEACEFUL HEART

Prayer begins by talking to God,
but it ends in listening to Him.
In the face of Absolute Truth,
silence is the soul's language.
FULTON J. SHEEN

No man is greater than his prayer life.
LEONARD RAVENHILL

You must go forward on your knees.
HUDSON TAYLOR

God's solution is just a prayer away!
MAX LUCADO

Is prayer your steering wheel or your spare tire?
CORRIE TEN BOOM

More from God's Word

These things I have spoken to you, that in Me
you may have peace. In the world you will have tribulation;
but be of good cheer, I have overcome the world.
JOHN 16:33 NKJV

The peace of God, which passeth all understanding,
shall keep your hearts and minds through Christ Jesus.
PHILIPPIANS 4:7 KJV

You, LORD, give true peace to those who
depend on you, because they trust you.
ISAIAH 26:3 NCV

You will keep in perfect peace
those whose minds are steadfast,
because they trust in you.
ISAIAH 26:3 NIV

Therefore, since we have been justified through faith,
we have peace with God through our Lord Jesus Christ.
ROMANS 5:1 NIV

A Timely Tip

God's peace is available to you this very moment if you place
absolute trust in Him. The Lord is your shepherd. Trust Him today
and be blessed.

81

PRAYING FOR DIFFICULT PEOPLE

PRAY FOR THOSE DIFFICULT PEOPLE

But I tell you, love your enemies
and pray for those who persecute you.
MATTHEW 5:44 NIV

Want an easy-to-use, highly reliable, readily available tool for dealing with difficult people? Well here it is: it's called prayer. You should pray for the difficult people in your life (as Jesus clearly instructed in Matthew 5:44), and you should pray for guidance in dealing with them.

Prayer is a powerful tool for communicating with your Creator; it is an opportunity to listen and to learn from the Giver of all things good. Prayer helps you find strength for today and hope for the future. Because prayer is powerful, it is not a thing to be taken lightly or to be used infrequently.

The quality of your spiritual life will be in direct proportion to the quality of your prayer life. Prayer changes things, and it changes you. Today, instead of turning things over in your mind, turn them over to God in prayer. Instead of worrying about the difficult people in your life, pray for them. Instead of fretting over your next decision, ask God to lead the way. Don't limit your prayers to meals or to bedtime. Pray constantly about things great and small because God is listening, and He wants to hear from you now.

MORE THOUGHTS ABOUT THE POWER OF PRAYER

*Any concern that is too small
to be turned into a prayer
is too small to be made into a burden.*
CORRIE TEN BOOM

*Two wings are necessary to lift
our souls toward God:
prayer and praise. Prayer asks.
Praise accepts the answer.*
LETTIE COWMAN

Prayer is our lifeline to God.
BILLY GRAHAM

*Don't pray when you feel like it.
Have an appointment with the Lord and keep it.*
CORRIE TEN BOOM

*It is impossible to overstate the need
for prayer in the fabric of family life.*
JAMES DOBSON

More from God's Word

Be anxious for nothing, but in everything by prayer
and supplication, with thanksgiving,
let your requests be made known to God.
Philippians 4:6 NKJV

Is anyone among you suffering? He should pray.
James 5:13 HCSB

Rejoice always, pray without ceasing, in everything give thanks;
for this is the will of God in Christ Jesus for you.
1 Thessalonians 5:16–18 NKJV

I desire therefore that the men pray everywhere,
lifting up holy hands, without wrath and doubting.
1 Timothy 2:8 NKJV

And whenever you stand praying, if you have anything
against anyone, forgive him, so that your Father
in heaven may also forgive you your wrongdoing.
Mark 11:25 HCSB

A Timely Tip

Prayer changes things, and it changes you. So pray. And if you're dealing with someone who possesses a difficult personality, pray for that person. God does not answer all of your prayers in the affirmative, but He does hear every prayer. So you must trust Him, whatever the answer.

82

PRIORITIES

FOCUS ON WHAT'S IMPORTANT TO
YOU AND YOUR LOVED ONES

Seek first God's kingdom and what God wants.
Then all your other needs will be met as well.
MATTHEW 6:33 NCV

First things first." These words are easy to speak but hard to put into practice, especially if you're dealing with difficult circumstances or difficult people. Difficult people have a way of captivating your thoughts and monopolizing your time. If you're not careful, you may find yourself focusing too intently on people and things that simply do not deserve so much of your attention. So what's the answer? Simple: you must learn to prioritize your time, even when prioritizing is hard.

If you're having trouble prioritizing your day, perhaps a major portion of your day has been hijacked by people who have managed to set priorities for you. And perhaps the priorities that have been set are not in your best interest. An important part of becoming a more responsible person is learning how to manage your time. Each waking moment holds the potential to do a good deed, to say a kind word, or to offer a heartfelt prayer. Your challenge, of course, is to use your time wisely in the service of God's kingdom and in accordance with His plan for your life.

So pray about your priorities. Then you can face the day with the assurance that the same God who placed the stars in the heavens will help you place first things first.

MORE THOUGHTS ABOUT PRIORITIES

Great relief and satisfaction can come from seeking
God's priorities for us in each season, discerning what is
"best" in the midst of many noble opportunities,
and pouring our most excellent energies into those things.
BETH MOORE

Each day is God's gift of a fresh unspoiled
opportunity to live according to His priorities.
ELIZABETH GEORGE

Energy and time are limited entities.
Therefore, we need to use them wisely,
focusing on what is truly important.
SARAH YOUNG

A disciple is a follower of Christ.
That means you take on His priorities as your own.
His agenda becomes your agenda.
His mission becomes your mission.
CHARLES STANLEY

More from God's Word

*Therefore, whether you eat or drink,
or whatever you do, do everything for God's glory.*
1 Corinthians 10:31 HCSB

*But prove yourselves doers of the word,
and not merely hearers who delude themselves.*
James 1:22 NASB

*Trust in the Lord with all your heart
and lean not on your own understanding.*
Proverbs 3:5 NIV

*Make yourself an example of good works
with integrity and dignity in your teaching.*
Titus 2:7 HCSB

For where your treasure is, there your heart will be also.
Luke 12:34 HCSB

A Timely Tip

Difficult people have a way of monopolizing your thoughts and re-prioritizing your life. But the ultimate responsibility for prioritizing your life is yours, not theirs. So it's up to you to establish your highest priorities (and to say no to requests that you simply don't have time for). Are you spending enough time on the most important things on your to-do list? If not, it's time to regain control of your calendar and your life.

83

PROBLEM SOLVING

PROBLEM SOLVING 101

People who do what is right may have many problems,
but the LORD will solve them all.

PSALM 34:19 NCV

Face facts: the upcoming day will not be problem-free. In fact, your life can be viewed as an exercise in problem solving. The question is not whether you will encounter difficult people or prickly problems; the real question is how you will choose to respond.

When it comes to solving the problems of everyday living, we often know precisely what needs to be done, but we may be slow in doing it—especially if what needs to be done is difficult or uncomfortable. So we put off till tomorrow what should be done today.

The words of Psalm 34 remind us that the Lord solves problems for "people who do what is right" (v. 19 NCV). And usually, doing "what is right" means doing the uncomfortable work of confronting our problems sooner rather than later. So with no further ado, let the problem solving begin...now.

More Thoughts about Problems and How to Solve Them

Every misfortune, every failure,
every loss may be transformed.
God has the power to transform
all misfortunes into "God-sends."
LETTIE COWMAN

Each problem is a God-appointed instructor.
CHARLES SWINDOLL

Human problems are never
greater than divine solutions.
ERWIN LUTZER

Faith points us beyond our problems
to the hope we have in Christ.
BILLY GRAHAM

Everyone gets discouraged. The question is:
Are you going to give up or get up? It's a choice.
JOHN MAXWELL

More from God's Word

I have learned in whatever state I am, to be content.
PHILIPPIANS 4:11 NKJV

Consider it a great joy, my brothers, whenever you experience various trials, knowing that the testing of your faith produces endurance. But endurance must do its complete work, so that you may be mature and complete, lacking nothing.

JAMES 1:2–4 HCSB

We are pressured in every way but not crushed; we are perplexed but not in despair.

2 CORINTHIANS 4:8 HCSB

We also have joy with our troubles, because we know that these troubles produce patience. And patience produces character, and character produces hope.

ROMANS 5:3–4 NCV

Trust the LORD your God with all your heart and lean not on your own understanding; in all your ways acknowledge him, and he will make your paths straight.

PROVERBS 3:5–6 NIV

A TIMELY TIP

There are two kinds of problems that you should never worry about: the small ones that you can handle and the big ones that God can handle. The problems that are simply too big to solve (like transforming another person's personality) should be left in God's hands while you invest your energy in things that you have the power fix.

84

PUTTING GOD FIRST

PUT GOD FIRST

You shall have no other gods before Me.
EXODUS 20:3 NKJV

For most of us, these are very busy times. We have obligations at home, at work, at school, or at church. From the moment we rise until the moment we drift off to sleep at night, we have things to do and people to contact. So how do we find time for God? We must *make* time for Him, plain and simple. When we put God first, we're blessed. But when we succumb to the pressures and temptations of the world, we inevitably pay a price for our misguided priorities.

In the book of Exodus, God warns that we should put no gods before Him. Yet all too often, we place our Lord in second, third, or fourth place as we focus on other things. When we place our desires for possessions and status above our love for God—or when we yield to the countless frustrations and distractions that surround us—we forfeit the peace that might otherwise be ours.

In the wilderness, Satan offered Jesus earthly power and unimaginable riches, but Jesus refused. Instead, He chose to worship His heavenly Father. We must do likewise by putting God first and worshiping Him only. God must come first. Always first.

More Thoughts about Putting God First

Jesus Christ is the first and last, author and finisher,
beginning and end, alpha and omega,
and by Him all other things hold together.
He must be first or nothing. God never comes next!
Vance Havner

Even the most routine part of your day
can be a spiritual act of worship.
Sarah Young

The most important thing you must
decide to do every day is put the Lord first.
Elizabeth George

God wants to be in our leisure time
as much as He is in our churches and in our work.
Beth Moore

Christ is either Lord of all,
or He is not Lord at all.
Hudson Taylor

More from God's Word

*Jesus said to him, "'You shall love the LORD your God
with all your heart, with all your soul, and with all
your mind.' This is the first and great commandment."*
MATTHEW 22:37-38 NKJV

*Do not love the world or the things that belong to the world.
If anyone loves the world, love for the Father is not in him.*
1 JOHN 2:15 HCSB

Be careful not to forget the LORD.
DEUTERONOMY 6:12 HCSB

*No one can serve two masters. For you will hate one and love
the other; you will be devoted to one and despise the other.
You cannot serve God and be enslaved to money.*
LUKE 16:13 NLT

*With my whole heart I have sought You; oh,
let me not wander from Your commandments!*
PSALM 119:10 NKJV

A Timely Tip

God deserves first place in your heart, and you deserve the experience of putting Him there and keeping Him there. So don't let difficult people or troublesome circumstances monopolize your thoughts. Put God first. When you do, everything else has a way of falling into place.

85

QUIET TIME

FINDING STRENGTH IN QUIET MOMENTS

In quietness and in confidence shall be your strength.
ISAIAH 30:15 KJV

The world seems to grow louder day by day, and angry people are using technology to spread negativity far and wide. No wonder our senses seem to be invaded at every turn. But if we allow difficult people or the distractions of a clamorous society to separate us from God's peace, we do ourselves a profound disservice.

If we sincerely want the peace that passes all understanding, we must carve out time each day for prayer and Bible study. When we meet with God in the morning, we can quiet our minds and sense His presence.

Has the busy pace of life robbed you of the peace that God has promised? If so, it's time to reorder your priorities and rearrange your schedule. Nothing is more important than the time you spend with your heavenly Father. So be sure to make a regularly scheduled appointment every day with your Creator. It's the perfect opportunity to be still and claim the inner peace that is found in the silent moments you spend with Him.

More Thoughts about Quiet Time

*God's voice is still and quiet
and easily buried under an avalanche of clamor.*
Charles Stanley

Nothing in all creation is so like God as stillness.
Johann Wolfgang von Goethe

*Strength is found not in busyness
and noise but in quietness.*
Lettie Cowman

*The world is full of noise.
Might we not set ourselves to learn
silence, stillness, solitude?*
Elisabeth Elliot

*I don't see how any Christian can survive,
let alone live life as more than a conqueror,
apart from a quiet time alone with God.*
Kay Arthur

MORE FROM GOD'S WORD

Now in the morning, having risen a long while
before daylight, He went out and departed
to a solitary place; and there He prayed.
MARK 1:35 NKJV

Listen in silence before me.
ISAIAH 41:1 NLT

Truly my soul silently waits for God;
from Him comes my salvation.
PSALM 62:1 NKJV

Be still, and know that I am God.
PSALM 46:10 KJV

To every thing there is a season…
a time to keep silence, and a time to speak.
ECCLESIASTES 3:1, 7 KJV

A TIMELY TIP

You live in a noisy world filled with distractions, interruptions, and occasional frustrations, a world where silence is in short supply. But God wants you to carve out quiet moments with Him. Silence is, indeed, golden. Value yours.

86

RENEWAL

HE CAN RESTORE YOUR STRENGTH

You are being renewed in the spirit of your minds;
you put on the new self, the one created according
to God's likeness in righteousness and purity of the truth.
EPHESIANS 4:23–24 HCSB

If you're continuously dealing with a difficult person—or if you're working inside an organization that makes unreasonable demands on your time—it's easy to become overcommitted, overworked, and overstressed. Before you know it, you may find yourself fretting 24/7, worrying about things that you probably can't change and almost certainly cannot control. What you need is time to reflect upon your circumstances and recharge your spiritual batteries. And one of the very best things you can do is to set aside time each day to spend a few minutes with your Creator.

God can renew your strength and restore your spirits if you let Him. But He won't force you to slow down, He won't force you to establish proper priorities, He won't force you to say no to the commitments you really shouldn't make, and He won't insist that you get enough sleep at night. He leaves those choices up to you.

If you're feeling chronically tired or discouraged—or if you're dealing with difficult circumstances that seem intractable—it's time to rearrange your schedule, turn off the TV, power down the phone, and spend quiet time with your Creator. He knows what you need, and He wants you to experience His peace and His love. He's ready, willing, and perfectly able to renew your strength and help you prioritize the items on your do-list if you ask Him. In fact, He's ready to hear your prayers right now. Please don't make Him wait.

More Thoughts about Renewal

God is not running an antique shop!
He is making all things new!
Vance Havner

The creation of a new heart, the renewing of a right spirit
is an omnipotent work of God. Leave it to the Creator.
Henry Drummond

God specializes in giving people a fresh start.
Rick Warren

Are you weak? Weary? Confused? Troubled? Pressured?
How is your relationship with God? Is it held in its place
of priority? I believe the greater the pressure,
the greater your need for time alone with Him.
Kay Arthur

Our Lord never drew power from Himself;
He drew it always from His Father.
Oswald Chambers

More from God's Word

*Therefore, if anyone is in Christ, he is a new creation;
old things have passed away; behold, all things have become new.*
2 Corinthians 5:17 NKJV

*Finally, brothers, rejoice. Become mature,
be encouraged, be of the same mind, be at peace,
and the God of love and peace will be with you.*
2 Corinthians 13:11 HCSB

*Those who hope in the LORD will renew their strength.
They will soar on wings like eagles; they will run
and not grow weary, they will walk and not be faint.*
Isaiah 40:31 NIV

*Remember ye not the former things, neither consider
the things of old. Behold, I will do a new thing.*
Isaiah 43:18–19 KJV

*Now the God of all grace, who called you
to His eternal glory in Christ Jesus, will personally
restore, establish, strengthen, and support you.*
1 Peter 5:10 HCSB

A Timely Tip

In every circumstance—even when you're trying to cope with an unfortunate situation or a difficult person—God is with you. He wants to give you peace, and He wants to renew your spirit. It's up to you to slow down and give Him a chance to do so.

87

SAYING NO

YES, YOU HAVE
THE RIGHT TO SAY NO

*Let us lay aside every weight, and the sin
which so easily ensnares us, and let us run
with endurance the race that is set before us.*
HEBREWS 12:1 NKJV

If you haven't yet learned to say no—to say it politely, firmly, and often—you're inviting untold stress into your life. Why? Because if you can't say no when it's appropriate, some people will take advantage of your good nature.

If you have trouble standing up for yourself, perhaps you're afraid that you'll be rejected. But here's a tip: don't worry too much about rejection, especially when you're rejected for doing the right thing.

Pleasing other people is a good thing up to a point. But you must never allow your willingness to please others to interfere with your own good judgment or with God's priorities.

God gave you a conscience for a reason: to inform you about the things you need to do as well as the things you don't need to do. It's up to you to follow your conscience wherever it may lead, even if it means making unpopular decisions. Your job, should you choose to accept it, is to be popular with God, not people.

MORE THOUGHTS ABOUT SAYING NO

Prescription for a happier and healthier life:
resolve to slow your pace; learn to say no gracefully;
reject the temptation to chase after more pleasures,
more hobbies, and more social entanglements.
JAMES DOBSON

As you live your life, you must localize
and define it. You cannot do everything.
PHILLIPS BROOKS

Learn to say no to the good
so you can say yes to the best.
JOHN MAXWELL

Efficiency is enhanced not
by what we accomplish but more often
by what we relinquish.
CHARLES SWINDOLL

You must learn to say no when
something is not right for you.
LEONTYNE PRICE

MORE FROM GOD'S WORD

*Obviously, I'm not trying to win the approval of people,
but of God. If pleasing people were my goal,
I would not be Christ's servant.*
GALATIANS 1:10 NLT

*The fear of man is a snare, but the one
who trusts in the LORD is protected.*
PROVERBS 29:25 HCSB

*Keep your eyes focused on what is right,
and look straight ahead to what is good.*
PROVERBS 4:25 NCV

*My son, if sinners entice you,
don't be persuaded.*
PROVERBS 1:10 HCSB

*Discretion will protect you and
understanding will guard you.*
PROVERBS 2:11 NIV

A TIMELY TIP

You can't do everything, which means that you need to learn how
to say no politely and often. Sometimes difficult people make
unreasonable requests, and when they do, you should decline their
requests without feeling guilty.

88

SELF-EXAMINATION

TAKE A LOOK IN THE MIRROR

*And why worry about a speck in your friend's eye when you
have a log in your own? How can you think of saying to your
friend, "Let me help you get rid of that speck in your eye,"
when you can't see past the log in your own eye? Hypocrite!
First get rid of the log in your own eye; then you will
see well enough to deal with the speck in your friend's eye.*

MATTHEW 7:3–5 NLT

All of us can be difficult to deal with at times. And all of us, from time to time, encounter folks who behave in the same way, or worse. If you have occasion to deal with difficult people (and you will), make sure that you're not the one being difficult. Perhaps the problems that concern you have their origin, at least partially, within your own heart. If so, fix yourself first (Philippians 2:3).

When you make a mistake, what's your attitude about it? Do you apologize to the people you've hurt, and do you try to fix things as soon as possible? And do you try to learn from your mistakes so that you won't repeat them? I hope so. Mistakes are a part of life. We all make them. The question is not *if* we will make mistakes; the question is what we choose to do *after* we make them.

Perhaps some important aspect of your life could stand improvement. If so, today is the perfect day to look closely at yourself and begin to make adjustments. When you do, you'll transform yourself into a living, breathing example of the wonderful changes that Christ can make in the lives of those who choose to walk with Him.

MORE THOUGHTS ABOUT SELF-EXAMINATION

The man who does not like self-examination may be pretty certain that things need examining.
C. H. SPURGEON

Face your deficiencies and acknowledge them; but do not let them master you. Let them teach you patience, sweetness, insight. When we do the best we can, we never know what miracle is wrought in our life, or in the life of another.
HELEN KELLER

Observe all men, thyself most.
BEN FRANKLIN

A humble knowledge of oneself is a surer road to God than a deep searching of the sciences.
THOMAS Á KEMPIS

Lord Jesus, let me know myself and know Thee.
ST. AUGUSTINE

More from God's Word

Wisdom is the principal thing; therefore get wisdom.
And in all your getting, get understanding.
PROVERBS 4:7 NKJV

Commit yourself to instruction;
listen carefully to words of knowledge.
PROVERBS 23:12 NLT

I urge you who have been chosen by God
to live up to the life to which God called you.
EPHESIANS 4:1 NKJV

Let the wise listen and add to their learning,
and let the discerning get guidance.
PROVERBS 1:5 NIV

And you shall know the truth,
and the truth shall make you free.
JOHN 8:32 NKJV

A Timely Tip

Sometimes you may be the person who is being difficult. This possibility may seem unlikely to you, but it is a possibility nonetheless. Consider it.

89

SEPARATION

WHEN YOU NEED DISTANCE

*Stay away from a fool, for you
will not find knowledge on their lips.*
PROVERBS 14:7 NIV

If you become involved in relationships that require you to compromise your values, you'll make yourself miserable. Why? Because when you find yourself in situations where other people are encouraging you to do things you know to be wrong, your guilty conscience simply won't let you be happy. And if you find yourself surrounded by people who are unstable, impulsive, or addicted, you'll soon discover that emotional distress is contagious, as are its consequences.

In a perfect world filled with perfect people, our relationships, too, would be perfect. But none of us is perfect and neither are our relationships...and that's okay. As we work to make our imperfect relationships a little happier and healthier, we grow as individuals and as families. But if we find ourselves in relationships that are debilitating or dangerous, then changes must be made, and soon.

If you find yourself caught up in a personal relationship that is bringing havoc into your life, and if you can't seem to find the courage to do something about it, don't hesitate to seek the advice of a trusted friend or your pastor or a professionally trained counselor. But whatever you do, don't be satisfied with the status quo.

To fully experience God's gifts, you need happy, emotionally healthy people to share them with. It's up to you to make sure that you do your part to build the kinds of relationships that will bring abundance to you, to your family, and to God's world.

More Thoughts about Protecting Yourself

You are justified in avoiding people who send you
from their presence with less hope and strength
to cope with life's problems than when you met them.
Ella Wheeler Wilcox

It is far better to be alone than to be in bad company.
George Washington

Not everybody is healthy enough
to have a front-row seat in your life.
Susan L. Taylor

Stay away from fatty foods, hard liquor, and negative people.
Marie T. Freeman

No one can drive us crazy unless we give them the keys.
Doug Horton

More from God's Word

Walk with the wise and become wise;
associate with fools and get in trouble.
Proverbs 13:20 NLT

Do not be deceived: "Bad company corrupts good morals."
1 Corinthians 15:33 HCSB

It is better to meet a bear robbed of her cubs
than to meet a fool doing foolish things.
Proverbs 17:12 NCV

You are not the same as those who do not believe.
So do not join yourselves to them. Good and bad do not
belong together. Light and darkness cannot share together.
2 Corinthians 6:14 NCV

Be sober, be vigilant; because your adversary the devil walks
about like a roaring lion, seeking whom he may devour.
1 Peter 5:8 NKJV

A Timely Tip

You can't change other people, but you can change the way that you react to them. If someone is threatening you, either physically or emotionally, you have the right to set boundaries and enforce those boundaries, even if it means separating yourself from that person.

90

SPIRITUAL GROWTH

SEIZE EVERY OPPORTUNITY
FOR SPIRITUAL GROWTH

*I remind you to fan into flames
the spiritual gift God gave you.*
2 TIMOTHY 1:6 NLT

Whether we realize it or not, the difficult people we encounter throughout life as individuals and as Christians we can—and should—never stop growing in the love and knowledge of our Lord. And, as individuals, we should never stop learning new and better ways to respond to all people, even the difficult ones.

When we cease to grow, either emotionally or spiritually, we do ourselves and our loved ones a profound disservice. But if we study God's Word, if we obey His commandments, and if we live in the center of His will, we will not be "stagnant" believers; we will, instead, be growing Christians, and that's exactly what God wants for our lives and our relationships.

Many of life's most important lessons are painful to learn. Thankfully, during times of heartbreak and hardship, God stands ready to protect us. As Psalm 46:1 promises, "God is our protection and our strength. He always helps in times of trouble" (NCV). In

His own time and according to His master plan, God will heal us if we invite Him into our hearts.

Spiritual growth need not take place only in times of adversity or pain. We must continue to grow, spiritually and emotionally, in every season of life. And whether we like them or not, difficult people have lessons to teach us that we could learn in no other way.

So if you're dealing with a difficult person, keep growing and keep praying. In those quiet moments when you open your heart to God, the One who made you will keep remaking you. He will give us direction, perspective, wisdom, and courage. And, the appropriate moment to accept those spiritual gifts is always the present one.

MORE THOUGHTS ABOUT SPIRITUAL GROWTH

God will help us become the people
we are meant to be, if only we will ask Him.
HANNAH WHITALL SMITH

Mark it down. You will never go where God is not.
MAX LUCADO

Grow, dear friends, but grow, I beseech you,
in God's way, which is the only true way.
HANNAH WHITALL SMITH

The vigor of our spiritual life will be in exact proportion
to the place held by the Bible in our life and thoughts.
GEORGE MUELLER

More from God's Word

*But endurance must do its complete work, so that you
may be mature and complete, lacking nothing.*
JAMES 1:4 HCSB

*Leave inexperience behind, and you will live;
pursue the way of understanding.*
PROVERBS 9:6 HCSB

*But grow in the grace and knowledge of our Lord and Savior
Jesus Christ. To Him be the glory both now and forever. Amen.*
2 PETER 3:18 NKJV

*And be not conformed to this world: but be ye transformed
by the renewing of your mind, that ye may prove
what is that good, and acceptable, and perfect will of God.*
ROMANS 12:2 KJV

*So let us stop going over the the basic teachings
about Christ again and again. Let us go on instead
and become mature in our understanding.*
HEBREWS 6:1 NLT

A Timely Tip

When it comes to your faith, God doesn't want you to stand still.
He wants you to keep growing. And sometimes He places people
along your path who, because of their personalities, can teach you
lessons you could have learned no other way. The Lord knows that
spiritual maturity is a lifelong journey. You should know it too.

91

STRENGTH

FINDING STRENGTH TO
DEAL WITH DIFFICULT PEOPLE

He gives strength to the weary,
and to him who lacks might He increases power.
ISAIAH 40:29 NASB

If you're dealing with difficult people—or if you find yourself working hard to extricate yourself from difficult circumstances—you need strength, and plenty of it. Graciously the Lord offers strength to those who ask for it. His strength is available to everyone, including you.

God's love never changes; neither do His promises. From the cradle to the grave, He has promised to give you the strength to meet any challenge. The Lord has promised to lift you up and guide your steps if you let Him. He has promised that when you entrust your life to Him completely and without reservation, He will give you the courage to face any trial and the wisdom to live in His righteousness.

God uplifts those who turn their hearts and prayers to Him. Have you "tapped in" to His strength? Have you turned your life and your heart over to Him, or are you muddling along under your own power? The answer to this question will determine the quality of your life, and it will also help determine how well you deal with difficult people. So start tapping into the Lord's divine power, and while you're at it, remember that when it comes to strength, He is the Ultimate Source.

MORE THOUGHTS ABOUT FINDING THE STRENGTH TO DEAL WITH DIFFICULT PEOPLE

God is in control. He may not take away trials or make detours for us, but He strengthens us through them.
BILLY GRAHAM

The truth is, God's strength is fully revealed when our strength is depleted.
LIZ CURTIS HIGGS

Faith is a strong power, mastering any difficulty in the strength of the Lord who made heaven and earth.
CORRIE TEN BOOM

God will give us the strength and resources we need to live through any situation in life that He ordains.
BILLY GRAHAM

The strength that we claim from God's Word does not depend on circumstances. Circumstances will be difficult, but our strength will be sufficient.
CORRIE TEN BOOM

More from God's Word

The LORD is my strength and my song;
He has become my salvation.
EXODUS 15:2 HCSB

Be strong and courageous, and do the work.
Don't be afraid or discouraged, for the LORD God,
my God, is with you. He won't leave you or forsake you.
1 CHRONICLES 28:20 HCSB

My grace is sufficient for you, for my power
is made perfect in weakness.
2 CORINTHIANS 12:9 NIV

Have faith in the LORD your God, and you will stand strong.
Have faith in his prophets, and you will succeed.
2 CHRONICLES 20:20 NCV

I can do all things through Christ who strengthens me.
PHILIPPIANS 4:13 NKJV

A Timely Tip

Need the strength to deal with a difficult person? Slow down, take a deep breath, collect your thoughts, and ask God for help...but not necessarily in that order.

92

STRESS

HOW TO MANAGE THE STRESS OF
DEALING WITH DIFFICULT PEOPLE

*Come unto me, all ye that labor and are heavy laden,
and I will give you rest.*
MATTHEW 11:28 KJV

There's no doubt about it: dealing with difficult people can be stressful. To make matters worse, we live in a stress-filled, media-driven world where stress-inducing messages are only a click away. So stressful days are an inevitable fact of modern life. And how do we cope with these challenges? The best place to start is by turning our days and our lives over to God. Elisabeth Elliot writes, "If my life is surrendered to God, all is well. Let me not grab it back, as though it were in peril in His hand but would be safer in mine!" Yet even the most devout Christian may, at times, seek to grab the reins of his or her life and proclaim, "I'm in charge!" To do so is foolish, prideful, and stress inducing.

When we seek to impose our own wills upon the world—or upon other people—we invite stress into our lives. But when we turn our lives and our hearts over to God—when we accept His will instead of seeking vainly to impose our own—we discover the inner peace that can be ours through Him.

Do you feel overwhelmed by the stresses of everyday life? Are you tormented by your interactions with a difficult person? If so, turn your concerns and your prayers over to God, completely and without reservation. He knows your needs and will meet those needs in His own way and in His own time if you let Him.

MORE THOUGHTS ABOUT MANAGING STRESS

There are many burned-out people
who think more is always better,
who deem it unspiritual to say no.
SARAH YOUNG

Beware of having so much to do that you really
do nothing at all because you
do not wait upon God to do it aright.
C. H. SPURGEON

Life is strenuous. See that your clock does not run down.
LETTIE COWMAN

God specializes in giving people a fresh start.
RICK WARREN

The more comfortable we are with mystery in our journey,
the more rest we will know along the way.
JOHN ELDREDGE

More from God's Word

*And the peace of God, which transcends
all understanding, will guard your
hearts and your minds in Christ Jesus.*
PHILIPPIANS 4:7 NIV

*You, LORD, give true peace to those
who depend on you, because they trust you.*
ISAIAH 26:3 NCV

I find rest in God; only he gives me hope.
PSALM 62:5 NCV

*Peace I leave with you; My peace I give to you;
not as the world gives do I give to you.
Do not let your heart be troubled, nor let it be fearful.*
JOHN 14:27 NASB

Live peaceful and quiet lives in all godliness and holiness.
1 TIMOTHY 2:2 NIV

A Timely Tip

If you're serious about beating stress, then you must form the habit
of talking to God first thing every morning. He's available. Are you?

93

TAKING RESPONSIBILITY

YOU'RE RESPONSIBLE FOR YOUR
BEHAVIOR (AND OTHER PEOPLE
ARE RESPONSIBLE FOR THEIRS)

But each person should examine his own work,
and then he will have a reason for boasting
in himself alone, and not in respect to someone else.
For each person will have to carry his own load.
GALATIANS 6:4–5 HCSB

It's time to state a rather obvious fact: you're responsible for your own behavior and other people are responsible for theirs. But if you're not careful, you may find yourself spending too much time worrying about the myriad ways that other people are misbehaving and not enough time focusing on your own responsibilities.

Trying to make difficult people behave themselves is a fruitless task: the job is never done, the working conditions are dreadful, and the pay is, more often than not, nonexistent. So instead of trying to improve other people, a better strategy is simply this: get busy trying to improve yourself.

God's Word encourages us to take responsibility for our actions, but the world tempts us to do otherwise. The media tries to convince us that we're "victims" of our upbringing, our government, our economic strata, or our circumstances, thus ignoring the countless blessings—and the gift of free will—that God has given each of us. We're also tempted to blame our problems on the people who make our lives difficult. It's an easy excuse, but a shortsighted one.

So who's responsible for your behavior? God's Word says that you are. That means you shouldn't waste time or energy blaming anybody else for your problems. The blame game has no winners; don't play.

More Thoughts about Taking Responsibility

We talk about circumstances that are "beyond our control."
None of us have control over our circumstances,
but we are responsible for the way we
pilot ourselves in the midst of things as they are.
Oswald Chambers

Man must cease attributing his problems
to his environment, and learn again
to exercise his will—his personal responsibility
in the realm of faith and morals.
Albert Schweitzer

Action springs not from thought,
but from a readiness for responsibility.
Dietrich Bonhoeffer

MORE FROM GOD'S WORD

So then, each of us will give an account of himself to God.
ROMANS 14:12 HCSB

By their fruits ye shall know them.
MATTHEW 7:20 KJV

Better to be patient than powerful;
better to have self-control than to conquer a city.
PROVERBS 16:32 NLT

Then He said to His disciples,
"The harvest is abundant,
but the workers are few."
MATTHEW 9:37 HCSB

We must do the works of Him who sent Me while it is day.
Night is coming when no one can work.
JOHN 9:4 HCSB

A TIMELY TIP

It's easy to hold other people accountable, but real accountability begins with the person you see when you look in the mirror. So don't look for someone you can blame; look for something constructive you can do. When you accept responsibility and take the necessary steps to resolve your problems, you'll feel better about yourself *and* you'll get more done. Lots more.

94

TEMPTATION

WHEN PEOPLE TEMPT
YOU TO MISBEHAVE

Do not be misled: "Bad company corrupts good character."
1 CORINTHIANS 15:33 NIV

If you stop to think about it, the cold, hard evidence is right in front of your eyes: you live in a temptation-filled world. The devil is out on the street, hard at work, causing pain and heartache in more ways than ever before. Yes, you live in a temptation nation, a place where the bad guys are working 24/7 to lead you astray. That's why you must remain vigilant. Not only must you resist Satan when he confronts you, but you must also avoid the people who encourage you to go places—or to do things—that are inconsistent with your faith.

In a letter to believers, Peter offers a stern warning: "Your adversary, the devil, prowls around like a roaring lion, seeking someone to devour" (1 Peter 5:8 NASB). What was true in New Testament times is equally true in our own. Satan tempts his prey and then devours them. It's up to you—and only you—to make sure that you're not one of the ones being devoured!

As Christians, we must beware because temptations are everywhere. Satan is determined to win; we must be equally determined that he does not.

MORE THOUGHTS ABOUT TEMPTATION

Every temptation, directly or indirectly,
is the temptation to doubt and distrust God.
JOHN MACARTHUR

The first step on the way to victory
is to recognize the enemy.
CORRIE TEN BOOM

Temptations that have been anticipated,
guarded against, and prayed about
have little power to harm us.
Jesus tells us to "keep watching
and praying, that you may not
come into temptation."
JOHN MACARTHUR

It is not the temptations you have,
but the decision you make about them, that counts.
BILLY GRAHAM

It is easier to stay out of temptation
than to get out of it.
RICK WARREN

More from God's Word

*No temptation has overtaken you but such
as is common to man; and God is faithful, who will
not allow you to be tempted beyond what you are able,
but with the temptation will provide the way of escape.*
1 Corinthians 10:13 NASB

*But encourage each other daily, while it is still called today,
so that none of you is hardened by sin's deception.*
Hebrews 3:13 HCSB

*Test all things; hold fast what is good.
Abstain from every form of evil.*
1 Thessalonians 5:21–22 NKJV

*Put on the whole armor of God, that you may
be able to stand against the wiles of the devil.*
Ephesians 6:11 NKJV

*Let us lay aside every weight, and the sin
which so easily ensnares us, and let us run
with endurance the race that is set before us.*
Hebrews 12:1 NKJV

A Timely Tip

It's an old saying and a true one: "When it comes to temptation, it's easier to stay out than it is to get out."

95

THOUGHTS

WHEN DEALING WITH DIFFICULT PEOPLE, GUARD YOUR THOUGHTS

Finally, brothers and sisters, whatever is true, whatever is noble,
whatever is right, whatever is pure, whatever is lovely,
whatever is admirable—if anything is excellent
or praiseworthy—think about such things.

PHILIPPIANS 4:8 NIV

How will you direct your thoughts today? Will you obey the words of Philippians 4:8 by dwelling upon those things that are honorable, true, and worthy of praise? Or will you allow your thoughts to be hijacked by difficult people, or by the general negativity that seems to dominate our troubled world?

Are you fearful, angry, frustrated, or worried? Are you so preoccupied with the concerns of this day that you fail to thank God for the promise of eternity? Are you confused, bitter, or pessimistic? If so, God wants to have a little talk with you.

God intends that you be an ambassador for Him, an enthusiastic, hope-filled Christian. But God won't force you to adopt a positive attitude. It's up to you to think positively about your blessings and your opportunities. So today and every day hereafter, celebrate this life that God has given you by focusing your thoughts and your energies upon things that are excellent and praiseworthy. Today, count your blessings instead of your hardships. And thank the Giver of all things good for gifts that are simply too numerous to count.

MORE THOUGHTS ABOUT THE POWER OF YOUR THOUGHTS

Change always starts in your mind.
The way you think determines the way you feel,
and the way you feel influences the way you act.
RICK WARREN

The things we think are the things that feed our souls.
If we think on pure and lovely things, we shall grow pure
and lovely like them; and the converse is equally true.
HANNAH WHITALL SMITH

It is the thoughts and intents of the heart
that shape a person's life.
JOHN ELDREDGE

When you think on the powerful truths of Scripture,
God uses His Word to change your way of thinking.
ELIZABETH GEORGE

Your life today is a result of your thinking yesterday.
Your life tomorrow will be determined by what you think today.
JOHN MAXWELL

MORE FROM GOD'S WORD

Set your mind on things above, not on things on the earth.
COLOSSIANS 3:2 NKJV

And do not be conformed to this world,
but be transformed by the renewing of your mind,
so that you may prove what the will of God is,
that which is good and acceptable and perfect.
ROMANS 12:2 NASB

The peace of God, which surpasses all understanding,
will guard your hearts and minds through Christ Jesus.
PHILIPPIANS 4:7 NKJV

Guard your heart above all else,
for it is the source of life.
PROVERBS 4:23 HCSB

For to be carnally minded is death,
but to be spiritually minded is life and peace.
ROMANS 8:6 NKJV

A TIMELY TIP

Difficult people have a way of hijacking your thoughts if you let them. Don't let them. Instead of focusing on the bad behavior of the difficult person, focus on your own blessings. And remember that life is far too short to allow a difficult person to derail your thoughts and harden your heart.

96

TODAY IS A GIFT

REMEMBER THAT
EVERY DAY IS PRECIOUS

So teach us to number our days,
that we may present to You a heart of wisdom.
PSALM 90:12 NASB

This day is a blessed gift from God. And as Christians, we have countless reasons to rejoice. Yet on some days, when we encounter difficult people—or when the demands of daily life threaten to overwhelm us—we don't feel much like rejoicing. Instead of celebrating God's glorious creation, we may find ourselves discouraged by the frustrations of today and worried about the uncertainties of tomorrow.

The familiar words of Psalm 118:24 remind us that "this is the day which the LORD hath made; we will rejoice and be glad in it" (KJV). So whatever this day holds for you, begin it and end it with God as your partner. And throughout the day, give thanks to the One who created you. God's love for you is infinite. Accept it joyfully...and be thankful.

More Thoughts about the Gift of Today

The one word in the spiritual vocabulary is now.
Oswald Chambers

Today is mine. Tomorrow is none of my business.
If I peer anxiously into the fog of the future,
I will strain my spiritual eyes so that
I will not see clearly what is required of me now.
Elisabeth Elliot

Yesterday is the tomb of time,
and tomorrow is the womb of time.
Only now is yours.
R. G. Lee

Each day is God's gift of a fresh
unspoiled opportunity to live
according to His priorities.
Elizabeth George

Faith does not concern itself
with the entire journey.
One step is enough.
Lettie Cowman

More from God's Word

This is the day the LORD has made;
let us rejoice and be glad in it.
PSALM 118:24 HCSB

Rejoice always, pray without ceasing,
in everything give thanks;
for this is the will of God in Christ Jesus for you.
1 THESSALONIANS 5:16–18 NKJV

So don't worry about tomorrow,
because tomorrow will have its own worries.
Each day has enough trouble of its own.
MATTHEW 6:34 NCV

Shout to the LORD, all the earth;
be jubilant, shout for joy, and sing.
PSALM 98:4 HCSB

These things I have spoken to you,
that My joy may remain in you,
and that your joy may be full.
JOHN 15:11 NKJV

A Timely Tip

Today is a wonderful, one-of-a-kind gift from God. Treat it that way. And as the day unfolds, don't let anyone rob you of the joy that can—and should—be yours.

97

UNDERSTANDING

PRAY FOR AN UNDERSTANDING HEART

*Teach me, O LORD, the way of Your statutes,
and I shall keep it to the end.*
PSALM 119:33 NKJV

What a blessing it is when our friends and loved ones genuinely seek to understand who we are and what we think. Just as we seek to be understood by others, so, too, should we seek to understand the hopes and dreams of our family members and friends.

We live in a busy world populated by fallible people who misbehave from time to time. When we're frustrated or upset by their behavior, it is all too easy to overlook their needs and motivations. But God's Word instructs us to do otherwise. In the Gospel of Matthew, Jesus declares, "In everything, therefore, treat people the same way you want them to treat you, for this is the Law and the Prophets" (Matthew 7:12 NASB).

Today, as you consider all the things that Christ has done in your life, honor Him by being a little kinder than necessary. Honor Him by slowing down long enough to notice the trials and tribulations of your neighbors. Honor Christ by trying to understand the needs and motivations of your friends and family members, even when they fall short of your expectations. As a follower of the One from Galilee, you should do no less.

More Thoughts about Understanding

*God will see to it that we understand
as much truth as we are willing to obey.*
Elisabeth Elliot

*Make it the first morning business of your life
to understand some part of the Bible clearly,
and make it your daily business to obey it.*
John Ruskin

*If we neglect the Bible, we cannot expect
to benefit from the wisdom and direction
that result from knowing God's Word.*
Vonette Bright

*The only way we can understand
the Bible is by personal contact
with the Living Word.*
Oswald Chambers

*Get into the habit of dealing
with God about everything.*
Oswald Chambers

More from God's Word

Morning by morning he wakens me
and opens my understanding to his will.
The Sovereign LORD has spoken to me, and I have listened.
Isaiah 50:4–5 NLT

Wisdom and strength belong to God;
counsel and understanding are His.
Job 12:13 HCSB

A foolish person enjoys doing wrong,
but a person with understanding enjoys doing what is wise.
Proverbs 10:23 NCV

A wise man will hear, and will increase learning;
and a man of understanding shall attain unto wise counsels.
Proverbs 1:5 KJV

Who among you is wise and understanding?
Let him show by his good behavior
his deeds in the gentleness of wisdom.
James 3:13 NASB

A Timely Tip

If you're trying to solve a difficult problem, you need wisdom: God's wisdom. Graciously, the Lord always makes His wisdom available to you. Your job is to acknowledge it, to understand it, and to apply it.

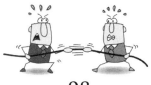

98

WALKING WITH JESUS

YOUR MOST IMPORTANT DECISION

For God so loved the world, that he gave
his only begotten Son, that whosoever believeth
in him should not perish, but have everlasting life.
JOHN 3:16 KJV

Every day, we're presented with countless opportunities to honor God by following in the footsteps of His Son. But we're sorely tempted to do otherwise, especially when we encounter people who possess prickly personalities.

Elisabeth Elliot had this advice for believers everywhere: "Choose Jesus Christ! Deny yourself, take up the cross, and follow Him, for the world must be shown. The world must see, in us, a discernible, visible, startling difference."

Today, do your part to take up the cross and follow Him, in a world that encourages you to do otherwise. When you're traveling step-by-step with the Son of God, you're always on the right path.

MORE THOUGHTS ABOUT WALKING WITH JESUS

At most, you will live a hundred years on earth,
but you will spend forever in eternity.
RICK WARREN

Death is not a journeying into
an unknown land. It is a voyage home.
We are not going to a strange country
but to our Father's house,
and among our kith and kin.
JOHN RUSKIN

Death is not the end of life;
it is only the gateway to eternity.
BILLY GRAHAM

Everything that is joined to the
immortal Head will share His immortality.
C. S. LEWIS

You need to think more about eternity and not less.
RICK WARREN

More from God's Word

*And this is the testimony: God has given us eternal life,
and this life is in His Son. The one who has the Son has life.
The one who doesn't have the Son of God does not have life.*
1 John 5:11–12 HCSB

*Therefore we were buried with Him by baptism into death,
in order that, just as Christ was raised from the dead by the
glory of the Father, so we too may walk in a new way of life.*
Romans 6:4 HCSB

*For the wages of sin is death, but the gift of God
is eternal life in Christ Jesus our Lord.*
Romans 6:23 NIV

*The Spirit of God, who raised Jesus from the dead, lives in you.
And just as God raised Christ Jesus from the dead, he will give
life to your mortal bodies by this same Spirit living within you.*
Romans 8:11 NLT

*"Follow Me," Jesus told them, "and I will make you fish for
people!" Immediately they left their nets and followed Him.*
Mark 1:17–18 HCSB

A Timely Tip

The ultimate choice, the most important decision you'll make in this lifetime, is the choice to invite God's Son into your heart. Choose wisely...and choose immediately.

99

WISDOM

TRUST GOD'S WISDOM

For the LORD gives wisdom; from His mouth
come knowledge and understanding.
PROVERBS 2:6 HCSB

Real wisdom doesn't come from talk radio, reality TV, the sports page, the evening news, or the Home Shopping Network. In fact, searching for genuine nuggets of wisdom in the endless stream of modern-day media messages is like panning for gold without a pan—only harder. Why? Because real wisdom doesn't come from the world; it comes from God...and it's up to you to ask Him for it. Consider these familiar words from the Sermon on the Mount:

> Ask, and it will be given to you; seek, and you will find;
> knock, and it will be opened to you. For everyone who
> asks receives, and he who seeks finds, and to him who
> knocks it will be opened.
> *Matthew 7:7–8 NKJV*

Jesus made it clear to His disciples: they should petition God to meet their needs. So should you. Genuine, heartfelt prayer produces powerful changes in you and in your world. When you lift your heart to God, you open yourself to a never-ending source of divine wisdom and infinite love. Yet too many folks are too timid or too pessimistic to ask God for help. Please don't count yourself among their number.

God will make you wiser if you have the courage to ask Him (and the determination to keep asking Him). But don't expect Him to do all the work. When you do your part, He will do His part—and when He does, you can expect miraculous results.

God has promised that when you ask for His help, He will not withhold it. So ask. Ask Him to meet the needs of your day. Ask Him to lead you, to protect you, and to correct you. Then trust the answers He gives.

More Thoughts about God's Wisdom

Knowledge is horizontal. Wisdom is vertical; it comes down from above.
Billy Graham

True wisdom is marked by willingness to listen and a sense of knowing when to yield.
Elizabeth George

Wisdom is the right use of knowledge. To know is not to be wise. There is no fool so great as the knowing fool. But, to know how to use knowledge is to have wisdom.
C. H. Spurgeon

More from God's Word

Get wisdom—how much better it is than gold!
And get understanding—it is preferable to silver.
PROVERBS 16:16 HCSB

But if any of you lacks wisdom, let him ask of God,
who gives to all generously and without reproach,
and it will be given to him.
JAMES 1:5 NASB

But the wisdom that is from above is first pure,
then peaceable, gentle, willing to yield, full of mercy
and good fruits, without partiality and without hypocrisy.
JAMES 3:17 NKJV

He that walketh with wise men shall be wise:
but a companion of fools shall be destroyed.
PROVERBS 13:20 KJV

Who among you is wise and understanding? Let him show
by his good behavior his deeds in the gentleness of wisdom.
JAMES 3:13 NASB

A Timely Tip

Need wisdom? God's got it and He wants you to acquire it. If you want the same thing, then study His Word and associate with godly people.

100

WORRY

TAKE YOUR WORRIES TO GOD, AND LEAVE THEM THERE

Cast all your anxiety on him because he cares for you.
1 PETER 5:7 NIV

If you find yourself in a difficult circumstance—or if you're caught up in a difficult relationship—you may find yourself trapped in a cycle of worry or regret. Jesus understood your concerns when He spoke the reassuring words found in the sixth chapter of Matthew:

> Therefore I say to you, do not worry about your life, what you will eat or what you will drink; nor about your body, what you will put on. Is not life more than food and the body more than clothing? Look at the birds of the air, for they neither sow nor reap nor gather into barns; yet your heavenly Father feeds them. Are you not of more value than they? Which of you by worrying can add one cubit to his stature?... Therefore do not worry about tomorrow, for tomorrow will worry about its own things. Sufficient for the day is its own trouble (vv. 25–27, 34 NKJV).

Where is the best place to take your worries? Take them to God. Take your troubles to Him; take your fears to Him; take your doubts to Him; take your weaknesses to Him; take your sorrows to Him...and leave them all there. Seek protection from the One who offers you eternal salvation; build your spiritual house upon the Rock that cannot be moved.

Perhaps you are concerned about your future, your relationships, or your finances. Or perhaps you are simply a worrier by nature. If so, choose to make Matthew 6 a regular part of your daily Bible reading. This beautiful passage will remind you that God still sits in His heaven and you are His beloved child. Then, perhaps, you will worry a little less and trust God a little more, and that's as it should be because God is trustworthy...and you are protected.

MORE THOUGHTS ABOUT WORRY

If we have our eyes upon ourselves,
our problems, and our pain,
we cannot lift our eyes upward.
BILLY GRAHAM

Knowing that God is faithful really helps me
to not be captivated by worry.
JOSH MCDOWELL

Worry is the senseless process of cluttering up tomorrow's
opportunities with leftover problems from today.
BARBARA JOHNSON

More from God's Word

Therefore do not worry about tomorrow,
for tomorrow will worry about its own things.
Sufficient for the day is its own trouble.
MATTHEW 6:34 NKJV

Do not be anxious about anything, but in everything, by prayer
and petition, with thanksgiving, present your requests to God.
PHILIPPIANS 4:6 NIV

Let not your heart be troubled;
you believe in God, believe also in Me.
JOHN 14:1 NKJV

Peace I leave with you; My peace I give to you;
not as the world gives do I give to you.
Do not let your heart be troubled, nor let it be fearful.
JOHN 14:27 NASB

Cast your burden on the LORD, and He shall sustain you;
He shall never permit the righteous to be moved.
PSALM 55:22 NKJV

A Timely Tip

Divide your areas of concern into two categories: those you can control and those you can't. Focus on the former and refuse to waste time or energy worrying about the latter. You have worries, but God has solutions. Your challenge is to trust Him to solve the problems that are simply too big for you to resolve on your own.

BIBLE VERSES ABOUT WORRY, FORGIVENESS, AND LOVE

Bible Verses about
Worry, Forgiveness, and Love

In dealing with difficult people, we must consider God's Word to be the final word. On the pages that follow, we reconsider three important concepts that play an important role in the way that we must deal with people who are tough to deal with.

When we deal with difficult people, we are tempted to worry about the things we've said, the ways that we've responded, and the implications that our interactions may have on future encounters. But the Bible instructs us *not* to worry about tomorrow. The verses that follow remind us to do our best and let God worry about the rest.

The Bible also instructs us to forgive the folks who have harmed us. So for Christians, forgiveness is not optional, and that's as it should be because forgiveness is its own reward.

Finally, God's Word has much to say about love. In fact, we are taught that God *is* love and that we must love our enemies, whether we want to love them or not.

So as you weave the concepts of this book into the fabric of your everyday life, try to worry less and love more. When you do, you'll make your corner of the world a better place, and that's precisely what God wants you to do.

BIBLE VERSES ABOUT WORRY

Worry weighs a person down.
PROVERBS 12:25 NLT

Though I walk through the valley
of the shadow of death,
I will fear no evil: for thou art with me.
PSALM 23:4 KJV

Be anxious for nothing,
but in everything by prayer
and supplication, with thanksgiving,
let your requests be made known to God.
PHILIPPIANS 4:6 NKJV

Humble yourselves, therefore,
under the mighty hand of God,
so that He may exalt you at the proper time,
casting all your care upon Him,
because He cares about you.
1 PETER 5:6–7 HCSB

Peace I leave with you,
My peace I give to you;
not as the world gives do I give to you.
Let not your heart be troubled,
neither let it be afraid.

JOHN 14:27 NKJV

Cast your burden on the LORD,
and He shall sustain you;
He shall never permit
the righteous to be moved.

PSALM 55:22 NKJV

Let not your heart be troubled;
you believe in God, believe also in Me.

JOHN 14:1 NKJV

I was very worried, but you comforted me.

PSALM 94:19 NCV

Therefore don't worry about tomorrow,
because tomorrow will worry about itself.
Each day has enough trouble of its own.

MATTHEW 6:34 HCSB

Bible Verses about Forgiveness

Hatred stirs up trouble, but love forgives all wrongs.
PROVERBS 10:12 NCV

Sensible people control their temper;
they earn respect by overlooking wrongs.
PROVERBS 19:11 NLT

If someone does wrong to you,
do not pay him back by doing wrong to him.
ROMANS 12:17 NCV

Bear with each other,
and forgive each other.
If someone does wrong to you,
forgive that person because the Lord forgave you.
COLOSSIANS 3:13 NCV

Get rid of all bitterness,
rage, anger, harsh words, and slander,
as well as all types of evil behavior.
Instead, be kind to each other,
tenderhearted, forgiving one another,
just as God through Christ has forgiven you.
EPHESIANS 4:31–32 NLT

If anyone claims, "I am living in the light,"
but hates a fellow believer,
that person is still living in darkness.
1 JOHN 2:9 NLT

See to it that no one repays evil for evil
to anyone, but always pursue what is good
for one another and for all.
1 THESSALONIANS 5:15 HCSB

And whenever you stand praying, if you have anything
against anyone, forgive him, so that your Father
in heaven may also forgive you your wrongdoing.
MARK 11:25 HCSB

You have heard that it was said, "Love your neighbor
and hate your enemies." But I say to you,
love your enemies. Pray for those who hurt you.
MATTHEW 5:43–44 NCV

Speak and act as those who are going to be judged
by the law that gives freedom, because judgment
without mercy will be shown to anyone
who has not been merciful. Mercy triumphs over judgment!
JAMES 2:12-13 NIV

Be merciful, just as your Father also is merciful.
LUKE 6:36 HCSB

BIBLE VERSES ABOUT LOVE

God is love; and he that dwelleth
in love dwelleth in God, and God in him.
1 JOHN 4:16 KJV

Love one another fervently with a pure heart.
1 PETER 1:22 NKJV

Though I speak with the tongues of men and of angels,
but have not love, I have become
sounding brass or a clanging cymbal.
1 CORINTHIANS 13:1 NKJV

Beloved, if God so loved us,
we also ought to love one another.
1 JOHN 4:11 NKJV

And may the Lord make you increase
and abound in love to one another and to all.
1 THESSALONIANS 3:12 NKJV

He who loves his brother abides in the light,
and there is no cause for stumbling in him.
1 JOHN 2:10 NKJV

Above all, put on love—the perfect bond of unity.
COLOSSIANS 3:14 HCSB

Live a life of love just as Christ loved us.
EPHESIANS 5:2 NCV

*But the fruit of the Spirit is love, joy, peace,
longsuffering, kindness, goodness, faithfulness,
gentleness, self-control. Against such there is no law.*
GALATIANS 5:22-23 NKJV

*You have heard that it was said, "Love your neighbor
and hate your enemy." But I tell you,
love your enemies and pray for those who persecute you,
that you may be children of your Father in heaven.*
MATTHEW 5:43–45 NIV

*This is My commandment, that you love
one another as I have loved you.*
JOHN 15:12 NKJV

*Love does no wrong to a neighbor.
Love, therefore, is the fulfillment of the law.*
ROMANS 13:10 HCSB

May mercy, peace, and love be multiplied to you.
JUDE 1:2 HCSB

*And now abide faith, hope, love, these three;
but the greatest of these is love.*
1 CORINTHIANS 13:13 NKJV

A FINAL NOTE

Not all people with difficult personalities have a diagnosable psychological disorder. But in some cases, folks with prickly personalities do suffer from conditions that can be treated by counseling or medication or a combination of the two.

For previous generations, mental illness was spoken about in whispers. For many sufferers and their families, emotional disorders were a source of embarrassment or shame. Thankfully, this is no longer the case. Today, mental health is a top-of-mind priority for medical professionals who are keenly aware that most mental disorders have both physical and psychological origins. Consequently, many emotional disorders are now eminently treatable. Thanks to advances in medical science, healing is available for those who seek it.

If you suspect that you—or someone you care about—may be experiencing a mood disorder, an anxiety disorder, a substance-abuse disorder, or any other psychiatric condition, don't hesitate to seek professional help. To fully experience God's abundance, you need to be spiritually and emotionally healthy. If mental health professionals can help you achieve the emotional stability you need to fully experience God's abundance here on earth, you should consider your treatment to be part of God's plan for your life.